GUNWHARF
QUAYS
PORTSMOUTH

Michael Underwood

TRICORN
BOOKS

GUNWHARF QUAYS

PORTSMOUTH

Gunwharf Quays
Portsmouth
Michael Underwood
Editor: Julie Underwood

Design © 131 Design
www.131design.org

Text © Michael Underwood
Images © Michael Underwood,
unless otherwise stated (see picture credits)

A CIP catalogue record for this book
is available from the British Library.

ISBN 978-1-909660-20-5

Published 2015 Tricorn Books
131 High Street, Portsmouth
PO1 2HW
www.tricornbooks.co.uk

Printed & bound in UK

Contents

Extract from land survey, HMS Vernon, 1980,
(showing Vulcan and Creasy buildings)

Introduction

Gunwharf Quays is a world-class shopping, leisure and residential development on Portsmouth's waterfront. Situated in a great natural harbour close to Portsmouth Historic Dockyard, its beautiful setting can rival any in the world.

Modelled on the phenomenally successful Victoria & Alfred Waterfront in Cape Town, South Africa, Gunwharf Quays provides an upmarket, upbeat venue. It has over 90 retail outlet stores, 30 bars and restaurants, a 14-screen cinema, an art gallery, casino, nightclub, a 26 lane bowling complex, fitness centre, marina and hotel. There are also over 500 dwellings, mostly in modern apartment buildings, the tallest of which is nicknamed 'the lipstick'.

Gunwharf has a fascinating history with its remaining old buildings beautifully conserved and in use today. Vulcan, the grandest of them, houses a restaurant, the Aspex contemporary art gallery and apartments.

The lively atmosphere at Gunwharf Quays, with large areas of waterfront cafés and promenade restaurants spilling out onto the terraces, continues late into the evening.

In contrast to many outlet centres, Gunwharf Quays is in the city, adjacent to the national rail, coach, bus and ferry interchange, and a short drive from the M27 motorway.

The uniqueness of Gunwharf Quays is striking, not only for the attractiveness of its waterfront setting but in the level of interest it generates. You can watch the comings and goings of Royal Navy ships, ferries taking passengers to France, Spain or the nearby Isle of Wight and, just across the harbour, to Gosport: the view is constantly changing. Take the lift up the iconic Spinnaker Tower, with its three viewing platforms (starting at 100m), for stunning views in every direction. The mood here today - relaxed, casual, fun - must be in stark contrast to how it would have been originally when it operated as a wharf for guns.

Over 300 years ago land was reclaimed from the harbour to build the first wharf, then 100 years later a second adjacent wharf, to store and maintain guns, cannon and all the accoutrements needed to arm Royal Navy warships and the army. By 1850 Portsmouth's gunwharf had become the biggest and grandest in the country, employing hundreds of men. From the late 19th century, Gunwharf, under the new name of HMS Vernon, was at the forefront of torpedo and mining warfare science and training, making a great contribution to the Second World War effort.

But, by the late 20th century, Gunwharf had become a sad reflection of its former glory. The semi-derelict, rat-infested site was put up for sale by the Ministry of Defence in 1996.

Vision

It is to the great credit of civic leaders at Portsmouth City Council, a local architect and a local land agent, that they had the vision to see that the old Gunwharf site could be regenerated for the benefit of the whole city by opening-up its greatest asset - the harbour - to the public. Changes in Government defence policy in the 1970s had led to many closures and redundancies in the armed forces and naturally 'Pompey' as the premier naval city, suffered in all this. Giving the waterfront back to the people would attract more visitors to Portsmouth, create inward investment and new business, and provide local jobs and a feeling of well-being for its citizens. The scheme produced, however, was not without its detractors who pressed for design changes and argued that more historic buildings should be retained.

In the end, hard work and commitment to the vision, with some modifications, attracted Millennium Lottery Funding of £40million towards the cost of the Renaissance of Portsmouth Harbour project, of which Gunwharf Quays was the lynchpin.

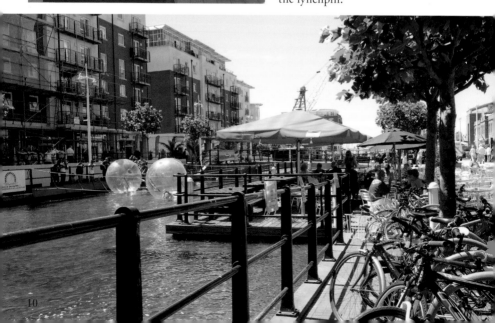

Construction

As a building operation, Gunwharf Quays was extremely complex. The site was tightly constrained by the sea, the railway station and track, and a ferry port. There were listed historic buildings that had to be retained and conserved and a great deal of demolition and excavation: a huge two-storey car park was excavated and built below sea level. Europe's biggest marine deck was constructed over part of the harbour creating more space for shops.

That the construction of Gunwharf Quays took less than three years from the start of demolition in August 1998 to the opening day on 28th February 2001 was an outstanding achievement.

Retail

As with the Victoria & Alfred Waterfront in Cape Town, the retail component at Gunwharf Quays comprises factory outlet stores where retailers fit out their store in the same way as their high street shops (enabling them to keep control of their brand) but selling their product at a minimum of 30 percent discount. Retail brands at Gunwharf Quays hold lease agreements based on performance.

The optimum mix of retail, leisure and residential units was required to ensure the success of Gunwharf Quays. The developers, Berkeley, and the city council had to work hard to convince retailers in Portsmouth and Southsea that a shopping complex at Gunwharf Quays would not harm, but benefit, their businesses by bringing more people into Portsmouth. But persuading potential retailers to take a risk by coming to a brand new development in a city that was not seen as a place for 'high end' shopping at that time proved to be very challenging.

Restaurants, bars, leisure

These were the most difficult businesses to attract to Gunwharf Quays - vital to create the 'festival atmosphere' of the vision. Rob Tincknell, commercial director for developers, Berkeley, visited waterfront sites around the world posing the questions: 'What would make Gunwharf Quays work and what would draw people to this development?' He knew that a vibrant leisure scene (a completely new concept to UK retail outlet centres) was fundamental to its success. His objective was to create 'a great day out' for which people would be prepared to travel a considerable distance: Gunwharf Quays itself would become a brand.

At first, potential tenants would 'walk away' when told there would be 28 other bars and restaurants on site. After two years no bar or restaurant units had been let. So, to illustrate what visitors to Gunwharf would experience, Rob began to arrange important client viewings when he knew an aircraft carrier was coming in. Tiger Tiger nightclub came first, then others followed.

Gunwharf Quays opened with a higher percentage of occupied retail lets than any previous factory outlet development in the UK: 85 shops; 20 bars and restaurants; a ten-pin bowling alley; a multi-screen cinema and a nightclub - a total of 250,000 sq ft on opening day. Others joined soon after to bring the total to 500,000 sq ft.

Preparing for opening 28 February 2001

Directors of Berkeley, including chief executive, Tony Pidgley, worked through the night sweeping, painting and clearing up, helping to get the site ready for opening the next day. In an inspired publicity stunt on opening day, the owner of Gunwharf's Pasty Presto, Steve Grocett, had some pasties hand-delivered to Chris Evans during his Virgin Radio Breakfast Show.

Marina

At the same time as Gunwharf Quays was being developed, Portsmouth's huge natural harbour was being marketed to establish it as one of the world's leading centres for yachting, maritime and water events. A marina with berthing facilities for tall ships was built at Gunwharf and major events brought in, including The Times Clipper Challenge, Whitbread Around the World Race, Cutty Sark Tall Ships Race, and the International Festival of the Sea. The events attracted thousands of visitors, benefiting the whole area around and across the harbour and generating worldwide publicity. In 2015 Sir Ben Ainslie, Olympic sailing champion, brought the America's Cup world class yachting to the harbour and established Ben Ainslie Racing (BAR) next to Gunwharf Quays.

Spinnaker Tower

In 2005 the 170m high Spinnaker Tower was completed and opened to the public. The design was chosen by the people of Portsmouth and the tower took four years to build.

Spinnaker attracts people from all around the world with breathtaking, panoramic views over Portsmouth's magnificent harbour, the historic naval dockyard, and up to 23 miles of constantly changing, uninterrupted views over land and sea.

Building a complex tower on such a restricted site in Gunwharf Quays, next to busy shops and restaurants and right by the sea, was an amazing achievement.

Right: Celebrating Gunwharf Quays' first anniversary in 2002
Below: Café in the Clouds at Spinnaker Tower

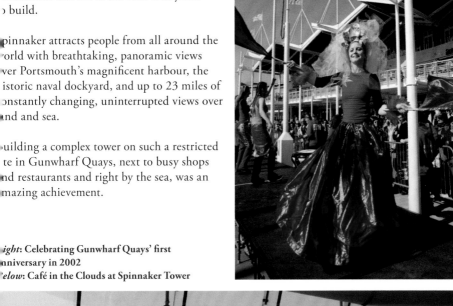

Ouze

The Point Street

Smock Alley

THE POINT

THE

THE

Round Tower

The Point Street

Eighteen Gun Battery

Sally Port

THE

Powe
Bi

**Plan of Portsmouth by Royal Engineer,
J P Desmaretz, 1750**

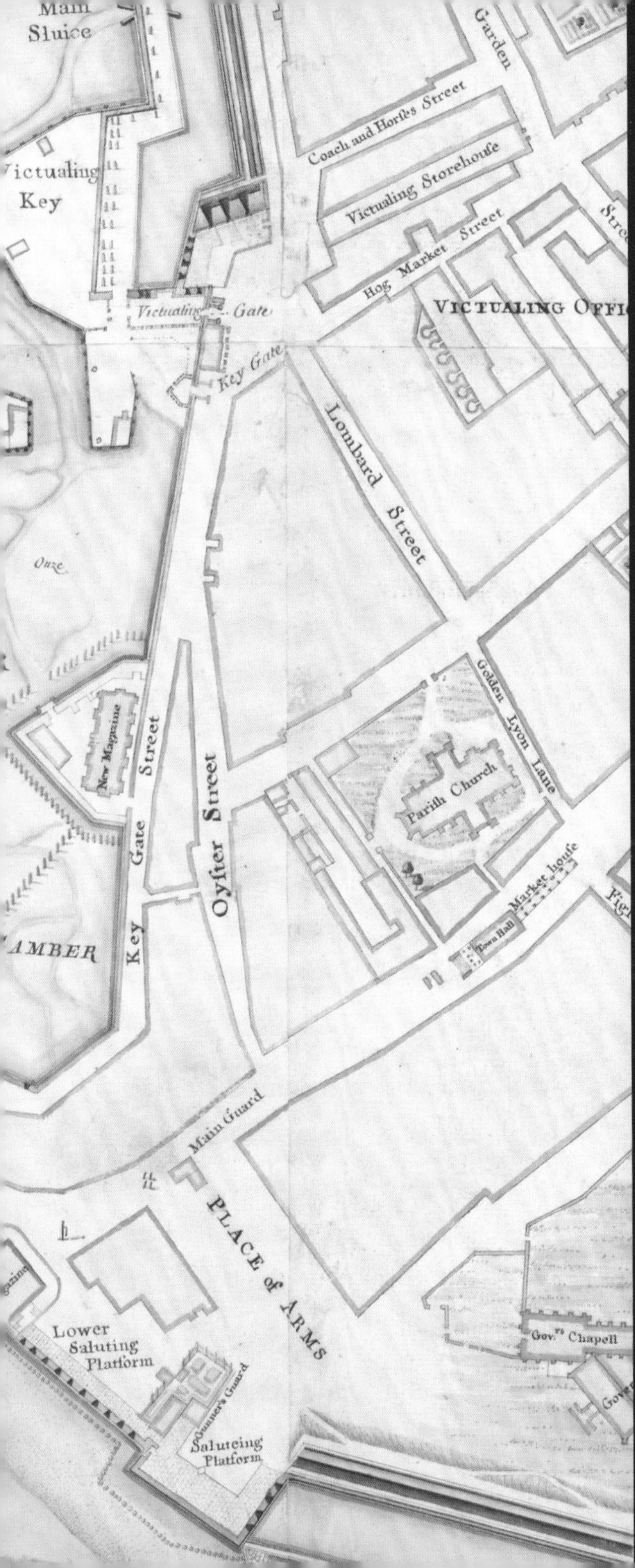

THE EARLY GUNWHARVES

1

The Royal Navy

'The Royal Navy was Henry's creation and it saved both himself and his daughter after him when they adopted an island policy and defied the catholic powers of Europe' Illustrated History of England, G M Trevelyan

Portsmouth's dockyard was established when Henry VII built the country's first dry dock in 1495.

Henry VIII's Navy

Henry's son, Henry VIII (reigning from 1509-1547), inherited five ships from his father, went on to capture 13 more, purchase 26, and build 46: 90 in all. Henry took a great interest both in his ships and in the newly established weapons they carried - his guns - and became known as the 'father of the navy'.

Despite the end of the Hundred Years War between England and France 1337-1453 there remained great animosity and the threat of naval attack from France and her ally, Scotland.

As a result, the young king ordered a programme of ship building and rebuilding at Portsmouth within the first two years of his reign, including constructing the *Mary Rose* (below). Fighting ships were now armed not only with archery but with guns and powerful cannon. The heavy guns were mounted on lower decks in Henry's ships, reducing the risk of capsize. They were able to fire devastating 'broadsides' through openings called gunports.

From 1512 Henry established additional dockyards on the Thames at Woolwich, Deptford and Erith, and at Chatham, on the River Medway, for his ever bigger ships. He also built a gunwharf at Woolwich. These new facilities had the advantage of being close to Henry's main residence at Greenwich as well as to the Tower of London, his and the nation's principal archery wharf and now its primary gunwharf.

Henry also constructed a chain of fortifications around the south-east coast of England, with Southsea Castle being built in 1544 to guard the eastern approach to Portsmouth.

The considerable administration required was conducted at the Tower of London as part of the Privy Wardrobe, one of the departments of the Royal Household. Henry established the Office of the Ordnance to look after his guns and the Navy Board to look after his ships.

Left: © Raphilena Bonito, 2014

The first gunwharf at Portsmouth

Although Henry VIII built new dockyards on the Thames, Portsmouth was still important to him

Henry realised the need to establish munitions storage at Portsmouth to equip his fighting ships on the south coast more efficiently. Neither of the fortifications guarding the harbour could be used: the Round Tower was unsuitable for munitions storage and the Square Tower was the residence of the Governor of Portsmouth. The new dockyard itself may have provided some gun storage but it is unlikely to have provided enough security.

Portchester Castle had already been used for munitions storage during the Hundred Years War. With its fortifications, keep and direct access to a quayside, it offered facilities and security similar to those at the Tower of London. However, it lacked adequate storage for big guns and in 1521 Henry ordered the building of a military storehouse over 70m (230ft) long and about 9m (30ft) wide. The outer bailey here was to be Portsmouth's first gunwharf.

The quay at Portchester Castle

storehouse in outer bailey, Portchester Castle

Outline of the military storehouse today

Town Quay: the second gunwharf

An opportunity arose for armament storage in town

The Navy grew under Henry VIII. In 1511 he presented a charter to Portsmouth and the town became a building centre for the king's ships. Nine acres (3.5 hectares) of reclaimed land were added to Portsmouth's dockyard in 1527, just as the munitions storehouse was being completed at Portchester.

Town Quay today

Later in the 16th century, during the reign of Elizabeth I and only a few years before the Spanish Armada, the Governor of Portsmouth moved out of the Square Tower to accommodation connected to the Domus Dei Hospital (Garrison Church). This provided an opportunity to transfer naval and military storage from Portchester to the Square Tower in Portsmouth, making operations more efficient. The Square Tower was adapted and became a munitions store for the next 190 years. At the same time the large storehouse at Portchester was demolished.

A wharf was needed to enable the transfer of guns and gunpowder from the Square Tower on and off the ships. As The Point was not yet developed, the wharf most likely to have been linked with these storage facilities was the town's quay ('The Key' on the plan). Located on the east side of The Camber, access to it from the Square Tower was wholly within the security of the town walls. The quay was accessible through a gateway in the wall. It seems that this quay was used for ordnance from around 1580 and became, for the following ninety years, Portsmouth's second gunwharf.

Overseas trade grew and in 1601 the (English) East India Company sent out its first ships. This developing merchant trade, in competition with the Dutch, was to lead to hostilities between the two nations.

Medieval Quay Gate

1580
WAS THE YEAR
Francis Drake arrived back in England with a rich cargo of spices and Spanish treasure, the first Englishman to circumnavigate the globe

At home, disputes between the incumbent king, Charles I, and the English Parliament led to the English Civil War (1642-9) and the establishment of a new form of government, the Commonwealth, under Oliver Cromwell.

The navy started to expand once more and by the early 1650s had doubled in size. There followed a series of naval conflicts and an increase in overseas territory requiring protection in which the navy, its dockyards and its gunwharves, played a considerable part.

Left: **Oliver Cromwell**
Right: **Key to Square Tower**

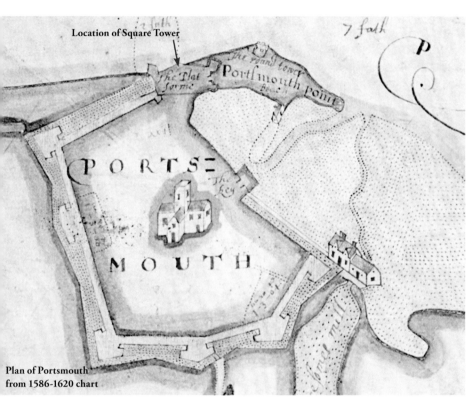

Location of Square Tower

**Plan of Portsmouth
from 1586-1620 chart**

The Square Tower, 1494

Portsmouth became the focus of a siege in 1642. Colonel George Goring had been made Governor of Portsmouth in 1639 and took the Royalist side in the Civil War. When the town was attacked from all sides by the Parliamentarians, Goring threatened to blow up the Square Tower with its 1,200 barrels of gunpowder unless he and his men were given safe passage out of Portsmouth. They were allowed to leave, but in parting defiance Goring threw the key to the Tower into the harbour. The dangers of having so much explosive within the town were underlined.

Peirson's wharf: the third gunwharf

By the 1650s The Point, the spit of land enclosing The Camber, had been developed with warehouses, other businesses, taverns and houses, and with streets such as The Point Street (now Broad Street) and Smock Alley (East Street). Here, at its northern tip, a wealthy shipowner, Nicholas Peirson, constructed a wharf and two storehouses with strong vaulted basement stores and living accommodation. In 1676 he leased the property to the Board of Ordnance for 99 years. This facility was used for guns, gun carriages and other stores but some gunpowder may have been stored there as well. Peirson's quay continued as an ordnance wharf for at least half a century and became Portsmouth's third gunwharf.

The town now had two principal munitions depots: the Square Tower (with its powder 'bridge' or pier) from 1716, and Peirson's quay. Although gunpowder supplies were brought down The Point Street from the Square Tower to Peirson's wharf rather than to the town quay, the hazards of storing and transporting munitions in the town remained.

The situation was exacerbated when another munitions store known as the New Magazine was built near the town quay. It was sited on a newly reclaimed, triangular promontory projecting from the town walls into The Camber. Land-fill for this extension started around 1690. High protective walls, with a sentry 'pulpit' (guérite) for extra security,

New Magazine, 1690s
© Raphilena Bonito, 2014

Left: Late C17 gun and carriage
Right: Peirson's wharf today

surrounded the magazine. This added a third munitions depot at Portsmouth - but here at least it was possible for gunpowder to be both loaded and off-loaded directly onto boats through gateways in its harbour walls.

Trade and wars

With the increasing affluence that new trade routes and colonies brought to England, the need for a stronger, better equipped, navy to expand and protect these acquisitions was evident. Growing hostilities with France added to the argument for a more powerful navy.

Right: Mural of The Point on wall of The Bridge pub overlooking The Camber

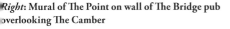

Plan of The Camber and The Point,
J P Desmaretz, 1743

Peirson's wharf

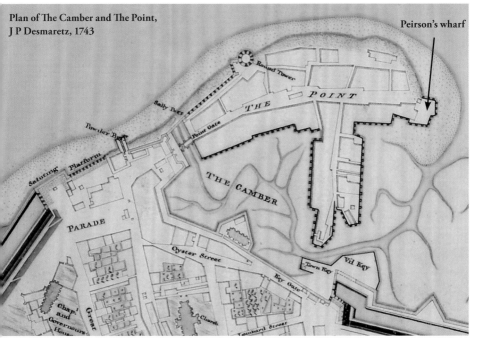

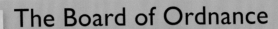

The Board of Ordnance

and other organisations concerned with gunwharves

This organisation, independent of the navy and army, was in control of the supply, manufacture and issue of the nation's munitions as well as the construction, maintenance, and operation of the nation's fortifications and gunwharves. Its symbol of a broad arrow and the letters B and O signified royal ownership and can be seen on guns, maps, plans, buildings and equipment.

Created by Henry VIII, the board's origins go back to the royal household department, the Privy Wardrobe, based at the Tower of London. Known first as the Office of the Ordnance, the board was responsible for the guns and other munitions kept at the tower and then at other arsenals, including Portsmouth.

The organisation was run by the Major-General, Lieutenant-General (until 1830), Surveyor-General, Clerk of the Ordnance, Clerk of the Deliveries of the Ordnance (until 1830), and the Storekeeper. The board used private contractors as well as its own factories.

There were two branches, the civil branch and the military branch. The civil branch was under the Surveyor-General and had six departments - manufacture (including gunpowder), defensive works, stores, contracts, land and survey (later becoming Ordnance Survey). The military branch comprised the Royal Engineers and, from 1683, the Royal Artillery. From 1812 the Royal Military Artificers (sappers and miners), the Royal Corps of Artillery Drivers, and, from 1741, the Royal Military Academy were also included.

The Board of Ordnance was disbanded in 1855, after poor performance in the Crimean War, and ordnance responsibilities went to the War Office. Early in the 20th century, an ordnance board was re-formed. Munitions matters now are the responsibility of Defence Munitions (based at Gosport and in Scotland), incorporating the work of former Royal Navy Armaments Depots such as RNAD, Priddy's Hard, Gosport.

Royal Engineers

Engineers, dating back to Norman times, were important in directing the construction of temporary and permanent fortifications, becoming especially necessary after the introduction of guns (working with the Royal Artillery). Both disciplines needed considerable technical knowledge and this led to the rise of the 'scientific officer'.

The Board of Ordnance established an officer Corps of Engineers in 1717 (Royal Engineers from 1787) with manual work being carried out by civilian artificer companies. The Royal Military Academy was established at Woolwich in 1741, again by the board, to provide necessary training.

The Royal Engineers were responsible for huge programmes of dockyard and gunwharf building works as well as the design of permanent fortification and temporary works on military campaigns, using the latest principles of European siege warfare.

Office of the Ordnance.

A Proportion of Ordnance, Carriages, Powder, Shot, Match, and other Amunition and Habiliaments of War, hereafter mentioned, to be prefently iffued out of His Majefties Stores, within the Office of the Ordnance, for fupply and furnifhing His Majefties *Shipp y. Kent . . . By Letter from y Lords of the Admiralty dated y 17 Decem: 1695*

Cannon of 7	
Demi-Cannon	22
24 pound Bullet	
Culverine	04
12 pound Bullet	

Above: A 'Proportion' (Order), dated 17 December 1695, from the Admiralty to the Storekeeper at Portsmouth to issue an extensive list of ordnance stores to HMS *Kent*. *Above right*: Board of Ordnance arrow on breech (rear end) of 16th century bronze gun

Royal Artillery

Guns were used by the English Army from the 14th century, but a permanent body of artillery was not formed until the early 18th century. Commonly known as the 'Gunners', the Royal Artillery continues to provide firepower to the British Army.

Royal Marines

Although the history of the Royal Marines goes back to the 17th century, it was formed as a body of marine infantrymen (soldier-seamen) for the Royal Navy in 1755.

The Royal Marine Artillery was founded in 1804 to operate artillery in bomb vessels (ships with mortars, short guns, bombarding shore positions with shells). The Portsmouth Royal Marine Artillery occupied the barracks at Gunwharf from 1824 until shortly after 1855. The Royal Marines are the UK's commando force and the Royal Navy's amphibious troops.

The Office of Works (also known as the King's Works)

This too had medieval origins within the Royal Household. The Office of Works was given responsibility for the construction and repair of royal residences, castles, fortifications and other royal estate matters.

By the 16th century the Office of Works was under the Surveyor to the King's Works, assisted by the comptroller and an increasing array of other officers (including Surveyor of the King's Private Roads, Royal Gardens and Waters, Paymasters, Architects, and Secretaries, and from 1609, a Lord Treasurer). A Board of Works was in control. There was also a team of artisans - bricklayers, joiners, plasterers, lock-smiths, carvers and many more, led by a Master Mason, a Master Carpenter, a Serjeant Plumber, a Serjeant Painter, and a Purveyor. The Office of Works became a nationally influential architectural and building department.

The 19th century office was overseen by a Surveyor General and administered public buildings, royal woods, forests and land revenues. After many further reorganisations it became the Ministry of Works and Buildings (1940), the Ministry of Works (1943) - set up to requisition properties for wartime use - then the Ministry of Public Buildings and Works (1962), and, finally, the Public Services Agency, under the Department of the Environment, from 1970 to 1990.

Today, each UK government department has its own works department, with the Royal Household continuing its historic responsibilities for the royal residences, Historic Royal Palaces (and HRP Enterprises Ltd) looking after major former residences, and Historic England, Historic Scotland and Cadw (the historic environment service in Wales) looking after most castles, forts and fortifications.

A. *The Queen's Yard and Dock*
B. *The Gun Wharf* .
C. *The Point* .
D. *The Magazine* .
E. *The Church* .
F. *The Governors House* .
G. *South Sea Castle* .
H. *Block House Point* .
I. *Charles Fort* .
K. *James's Fort* .
L. *Gosport* .

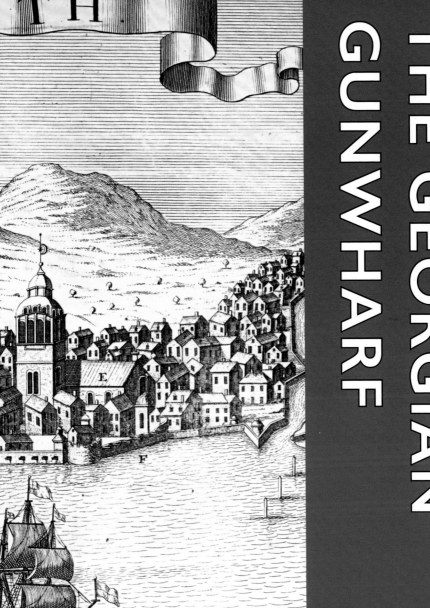

From Perspective View, 1710

THE GEORGIAN GUNWHARF

2

27

'Another wharf built particularly for the guns'

The fourth gunwharf

In 1699 the Board of Ordnance reported 'the wharf [Peirson's] where our guns lie is not in very good condition .... it might be better to have another wharf built particularly for the guns'.

The 1688 Glorious Revolution led to a growing alliance between England and Holland against attempts by France's King Louis XIV to regain England for James II. This initiated wars with France for over a hundred years. A peace treaty of 1697 was indecisive and war broke out regularly until English victories at the battles of Trafalgar and Waterloo in the early 19th century.

Expansion of Dockyards

Wars and threats of wars brought about further expansion of the Royal Navy with a new 1690s dockyard at Plymouth and expansions at Chatham and Portsmouth.

Expansion of Gunwharves

At Portsmouth the problems of insufficient and unsuitable munitions storage and powder locations persisted. Initially it was thought that a new gunwharf could be built in The Camber near Peirson's quay. However, William Boulter, Assistant Surveyor at the Office of Ordnance, considered that it 'must be erected on that part of the Ouze between high and low watermark that lies nearest to the mill'. A cheaper proposal by the board for a wharf at Blockhouse Point (on the Gosport side of the harbour) was overruled by the Admiralty.

Financial constraints meant building a new gunwharf was put on hold for several years, after which a decision was made to proceed with the scheme near the mill. This would be the first 'planned' gunwharf in the country.

Reclaiming the land

Before any building work could begin, land had to be reclaimed from the mudflats for what was to become the fourth gunwharf at Portsmouth. Reclamation was underway in 1707.

Quay walls were set out following the perimeter lines of revised Board of Ordnance plans; the stonework being laid section by section on timber piles. Then the site area within the quay walls was progressively built up with soil and gravel excavated from areas east of the dockyard within what was known as West Docke Fields, later The Common and later still the dock-workers' town, Portsea. The wharf was positioned between the mill-pond creek and a creek further north, maximising water depth along the sides.

By around 1714 reclamation had been completed and many of the necessary buildings erected or under construction.

Bishop Street, Portsea

1694

WAS THE YEAR the Bank of England was founded to fund William III's naval (and other) wars - creating the concept of the 'National Debt'

The Old Shakespeare's Head

A huge army of workers was recruited for the excavation and backfilling operations and were paid in a pub in Bishop Street known as the Old Shakespeare's Head after the contractor, a Mr William Shakespeare.

Left: William III and Mary (1689-1702): Protestant Prince William of Orange, was invited to England to become King. His wife Mary, daughter of James II, became Queen.
Right: Blockhouse Point, Gosport

Outline of the built design (jutting out towards the low watermark) added to the plan later, c1706

Original gunwharf proposal with a long curved quay served by a channel cut into the ouze, storehouses and small guard lodges

▲ Board of Ordnance Plan, 1700, produced to show proposals for a new gunwharf

29

Planned gunwharves

The need for better gunwharf provision led to a new concept: purpose-designed or 'planned' gunwharves

Ad hoc arrangements such as those in Portsmouth at the end of the 17th century just would not do; planned gunwharves, carefully designed and properly constructed, became essential. These matters occupied the minds of the engineers of the Board of Ordnance in the early decades of the 18th century; the designs for their storehouses and other buildings were inspired by the muscular 'castle-air' architecture of John Vanbrugh and Nicholas Hawksmoor at the Office of Works and the design legacy of Christopher Wren.

The first designed gunwharf

The new gunwharf at Portsmouth (built c1707-1715) was the first purpose-designed example in the country and consequently, fulfilled all requirements. It was followed by others: Chatham (c1717), and Morice Yard (1719-25) at Plymouth dockyard (later known as Devonport).

Planning Gunwharves

The requirements for an efficient gun wharf for the new century were:

- **a convenient location** near the dockyard

- **a good deep-water wharf** for hoys (sailing barges) and other supply craft

- **storehouses** for gun carriages, powder horns, cartridges, tallow, oil and other provisions

- **workshops** for making and repairing gun carriages, guns and other equipment

Below: Drawing instruments

Part of plan of Portsmouth and its fortifications showing the new 'Gunwharfe' by J P Desmaretz, 1750

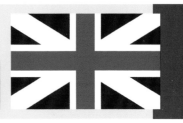

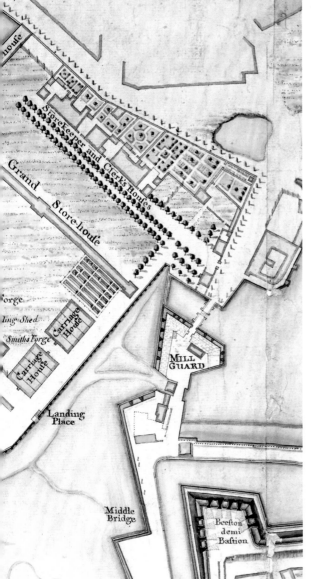

Above left to right:
Powder horn; Royal Military Academy; Union Flag

- **officers' accommodation,** administrative offices and living quarters
- **good security** - a substantial wall with guarded entrance gates
- **gunpowder storage** - safely on site or nearby

1720

WAS THE YEAR
the Royal Military Academy, Woolwich, (above) was built (attributed to Vanbrugh). It also housed the board room for officers of the ordnance

Stephen Martin-Leake, a navy pay office clerk, wrote in 1729:

'The Ordnance is a pretty neat place; it runs west into the harbour, just beyond the Mill Gate, flanking the covert way. Here they have a line of guns upon land carriages which they fire upon rejoicing days and hoist the Union* flag upon a tall flagstaff.' (*the new union between England and Scotland, dated 1707)

Labels on map: houſe, Storekeeper and Clerks Houſes, Grand Store-houſe, orge, ing Shed, Smiths Forge, Carriage Houſe, Carriage Houſe, Landing Place, MILL GUARD, Middle Bridge, Beeſton demi Baſtion

31

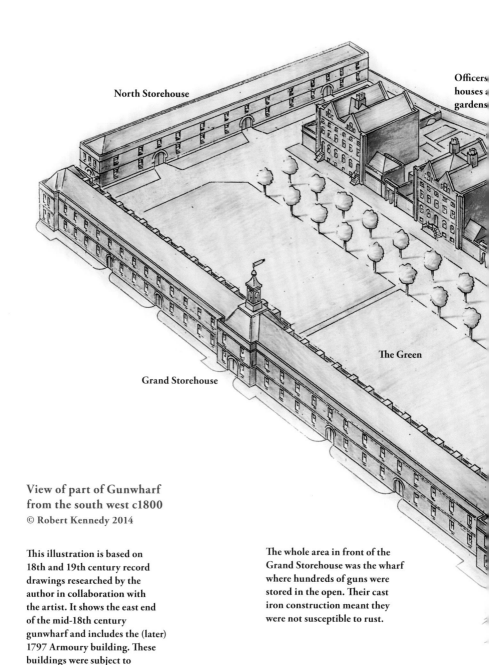

North Storehouse

Officers[
houses [
gardens[

The Green

Grand Storehouse

View of part of Gunwharf from the south west c1800
© Robert Kennedy 2014

This illustration is based on 18th and 19th century record drawings researched by the author in collaboration with the artist. It shows the east end of the mid-18th century gunwharf and includes the (later) 1797 Armoury building. These buildings were subject to constant alteration and some details included are of a later date; some minor buildings have been omitted.

The whole area in front of the Grand Storehouse was the wharf where hundreds of guns were stored in the open. Their cast iron construction meant they were not susceptible to rust.

The Common (later, Portsea)

Boundary wall

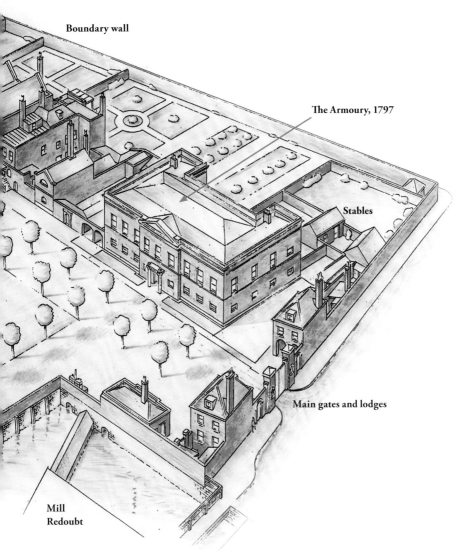

The Armoury, 1797

Stables

Main gates and lodges

Mill
Redoubt

33

The Grand Storehouse

The longest ordnance storehouse in the country

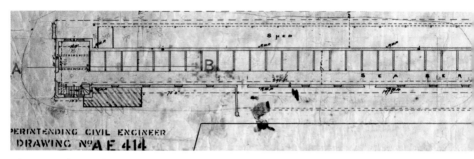

The Grand Storehouse was built between 1710 and 1715. The original 1700 plan for the Portsmouth gunwharf (earlier in this section) suggests that a Dutch-style quadrangular storehouse was the initial idea. But what emerged when the revised polygonal gunwharf was constructed was a storehouse of extraordinary length, at 150m (491ft) the longest ordnance storehouse ever built in this country.

Late 19th century record drawings show that it had classically inspired parapets but steep pitched roofs, reminiscent of Dutch influenced buildings, to the attic storage accommodation.

The storehouse was remarkably narrow (just 6m, 20ft, externally); each floor had access along one side to storage bays on the other. Staircases were in wider pavilions at the end and the centre. The building had a delicate central tower probably for a clock. Dormer windows at roof level faced The Green and the officers' houses (rather than the harbour) to add architectural interest to the more public side of the gunwharf.

The slightly later 18th century ordnance storehouses at Chatham and Plymouth displayed a more robust style. The grim Chatham building, 106m (347ft) long but nearly twice the width of its Portsmouth counterpart, was a particularly good example of architecture inspired by Hawksmoor and Vanbrugh, with great military towers rather than quiet pavilions.

The pair of storehouses at Morice Yard, Devonport (Plymouth), are the only remaining ordnance storehouses of this period. By the mid-19th century the Portsmouth building by then known as Sea Service Store No. 2 had been shortened at the south end. It was demolished around 1920 to make way for new buildings for HMS Vernon.

Chatham Ordnance Storehouse, 1717

1714

WAS THE YEAR
George I came to the throne. It was the start of the Georgian period of English history and architecture

1720

WAS THE YEAR
huge fortunes were lost when the South Sea bubble burst triggering a major financial crash in the City of London

Location

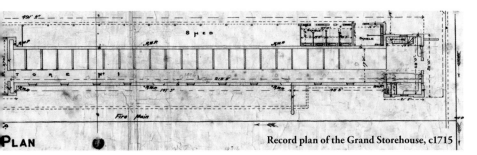

PLAN

Record plan of the Grand Storehouse, c1715

The North Storehouse was an additional contemporary storehouse, 67m (220ft) long and 6m (20ft) wide, alongside the northern wall.

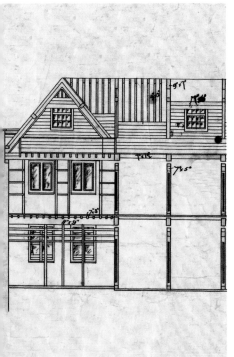

Section at north end of Grand Storehouse

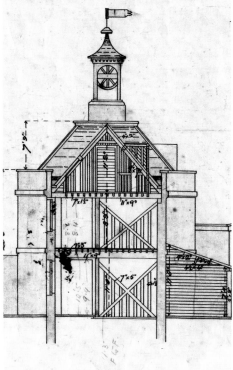

Cross section through Grand Storehouse

Officers' quarters

*An impressive symmetrical group of houses and
quarters for the Storekeeper, his assistant
and their team of clerks*

Designed in three blocks, the quarters were built in brick, with the central building approximately on the principal axis of the Grand Storehouse. They were completed by around 1720 - although modified extensively in later years.

The largest property, nearest the gate (House No 1 on the plan below), was the residence of the Storekeeper. He had a senior position under the Major-General,

Ordnance, Portsmouth, and was responsible for the security, care, maintenance, supply and receipt of all ordnance stores on the site. The Storekeeper and his team all had military ranks.

These quarters were substantially affected by the construction of the Portsmouth Harbour railway in 1876 and were finally swept away during redevelopment in the 1920s when HMS Vernon came ashore.

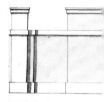

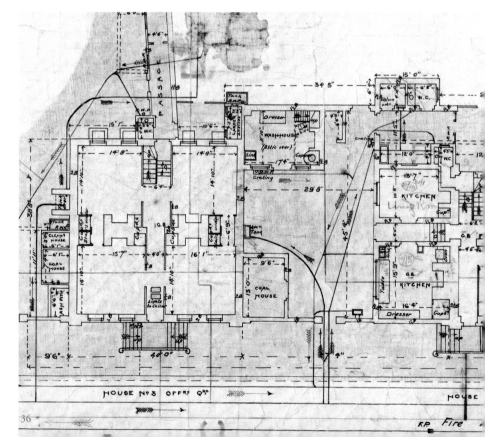

HOUSE Nº 3 OFFRS QRS

HOUSE

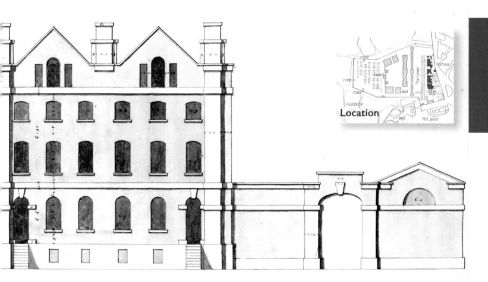

Location

Above: 'Houses for the Storekeeper and his Clerke at the Gunwharfe, Portsmouth, 1717'

Below: Record drawing of two of the three blocks, 1872. The buildings have been altered and extended significantly from their original form

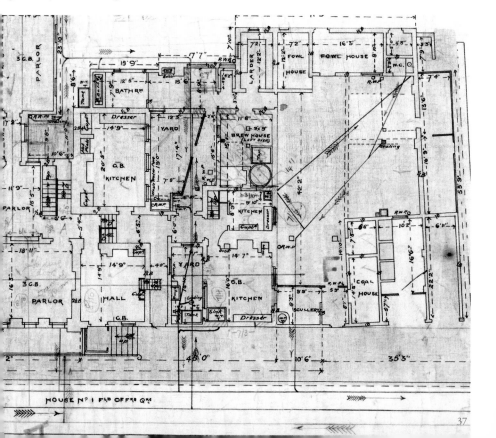

Carriage stores, forges, cranes and guns

This was the working area for the storage, repair, supply and receipt of guns - the prime purpose of a gun wharf

Gun carriage stores

Two pairs of identical gun carriage houses were built on either side of the tapering wharf west of the Grand Storehouse. Each building had five bays (sections), with double doors front and back, and were originally single storey with simple timber king-post roof trusses.

Over the years there were many modifications and the 9m (30ft) gap between each pair of stores was filled in and roofed over for more accommodation. The northern pair continued to store gun carriages until they were rebuilt between 1887 and 1889 as two-storey stores for barrack and hospital equipment.

A second storey was added to the southern pair which became offices and stores, and by 1900 the western building was a harness store and the eastern building was for 'in-packages' and general storage. Prior to demolition in 1998 some lower brickwork, probably dating from the 18th century, could still be seen.

Guns made of cast iron were stored in the open air; unlike wrought iron, this material is not susceptible to rust.

1 1750 plan detail. Note pyramids of shot stored in front of storehouse
2 North and south carriage stores (red) on 1860 plan

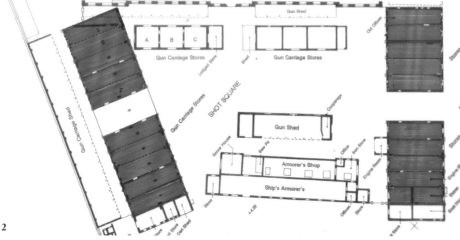

2

3

4

- South Carriage Stores (Hecla building) awaiting demolition in 1997
  Guns (1747) cast at Woolwich
- Timber cranes similar to this one at Guildford would have loaded guns, carriages and shot from the wharf onto sailing barges (hoys) at Gunwharf
- Forges similar to this one at Southsea were used in making and repairing ironwork for guns, carriages and other munitions
- Part of Portsmouth Storekeeper's inventory, 1715

5

6

7

		Serv[bl]	Repair	unserv[bl]
	24 Pounders	25		
	Demy Culvering	00		
	3 Pounders	65		
	Halfcunett		02	
	Halfcunett wth Swivells		04	
	Rabonett		01	
	Cannon of 7			
	Demi-Cannon		82	
	24 pound Bullet		13	

Spare Brasse Ordnance

Walls and gates

Gunwharf was a major new facility and had an impressive gateway to suit

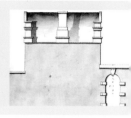

A 3.5m (12ft) high brick wall secured the east and south boundaries of the gunwharf. Running alongside Ordnance Row, it formed the rear boundary wall to the officers' gardens before turning westwards towards the King's Mill. The main gates were in this final short section.

The 3.5m wide gateway was flanked by two substantial brick piers with stone caps. Smaller arched doorways for pedestrians were provided in the walls on either side of the piers. Inside, and backing onto the walls, were two, four-storey lodges; one for the Foreman and the other for the Police Sergeant.

Each lodge had a yard with washroom, toilet and coal store; stabling was attached to the Foreman's yard. Both had a porch guarding the entrance gates and there was a small office kiosk on the Sergeant's side.

This gateway with its tall and extensive lodge accommodation (complete with even higher chimneys) was, apart from minor details, symmetrically planned.

Gunwharf gates and lodges viewed from the road to the dockyard
© Raphilena Bonito 2014

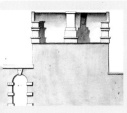

Left: Design drawing of wall and lodges (not as built), 1717
Below right: Record plan of 18th century lodges (ground floor), wall and gates, 1872

Location

Record drawing of one of the 18th century lodges, 1872

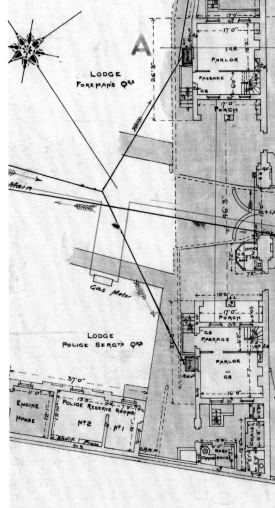

Fine new buildings for Gunwharf

*Portsmouth's gunwharf in 1720 was
the best in the country*

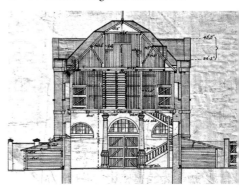

Artillery store, c1780s

Military success in Europe culminated in the Peace of Utrecht in 1713, enabling 18th century Britain to grow into a major world economic power. The population more than doubled, and, despite wars with France, overall the threat of war in Europe reduced. Trade in gold, silver, slaves, spices, sugar, furs and tobacco from new colonies and commercial interests in the Americas, West Africa, India and the Far East fuelled this economic growth. At home, later in the century, the onset of the industrial revolution began transforming the economy while generating social upheaval.

The Royal Navy had a stellar role in protecting Britain's maritime trade - not least from piracy, which was rife - and the British public came to be proud of it and its traditions. Britain became the 'empire of the seas'. Many fine naval buildings were erected reflecting not only the navy's physical needs but also its national status.

Gunwharf was consolidated with additional storehouses, particularly as the lease on Peirson's quay had come to an end. A large artillery store (c1780) and a fine armoury

(1797) were built. Cutlasses, boarding pikes, pistols, long-barrelled muskets as well as the wide range of necessary accoutrements all required storage space.

Powder storage remained at the Square Tower until around 1777 when it was transferred across the harbour to a new magazine at Priddy's Hard, Gosport. Some powder storage had continued at The Camber magazine until 1764.

Above: **Artillery Store Section**
Below: **plan based on 1861 drawing of former 1780 Artillery Store, west of Grand Storehouse (Sea Service Store No 2). The gun carriage stores are 19th century**

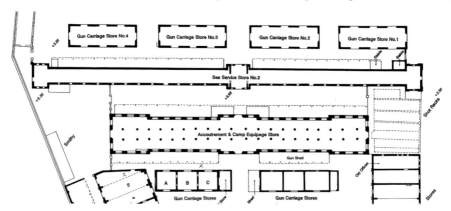

Location

During this period there was much development at the dockyard itself: new docks, storehouses and the Royal Naval Academy. Across the harbour, Haslar Hospital was established by 1746 and Weovil's yard was increasingly used for victualling supplies, becoming Royal Clarence Yard in 1831.

1740
WAS THE YEAR
when the song 'Rule Britannia' was first sung

Rule Britannia

Armoury, 1797, photographed c1900

18th Century Sea Service Pattern Musket (Brown Bess)

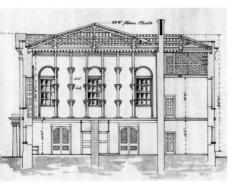

Armoury Section showing racks for guns at first floor

1799
WAS THE YEAR
Income Tax was first introduced (to fund the wars)

Pistols used for hand-to-hand fighting on ships

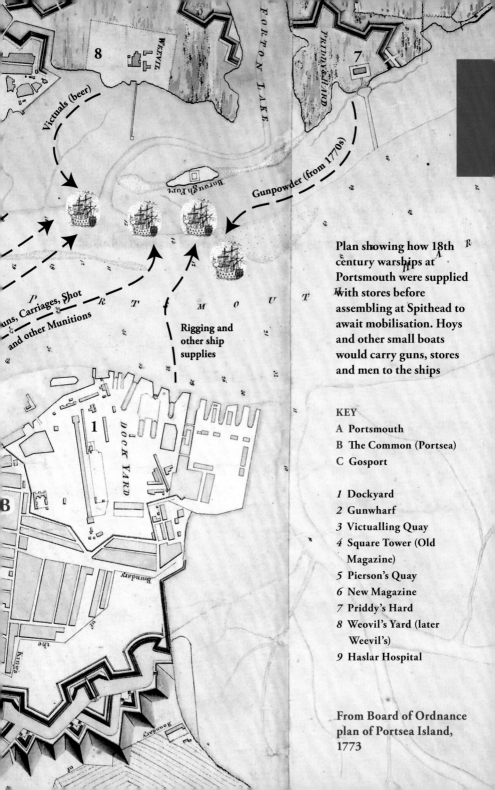

Victuals (beer)

Gunpowder (from 1770s)

Guns, Carriages, Shot
and other Munitions

Rigging and
other ship
supplies

Plan showing how 18th
century warships at
Portsmouth were supplied
with stores before
assembling at Spithead to
await mobilisation. Hoys
and other small boats
would carry guns, stores
and men to the ships

KEY
A Portsmouth
B The Common (Portsea)
C Gosport

1 Dockyard
2 Gunwharf
3 Victualling Quay
4 Square Tower (Old
   Magazine)
5 Pierson's Quay
6 New Magazine
7 Priddy's Hard
8 Weovil's Yard (later
   Weovil's)
9 Haslar Hospital

From Board of Ordnance
plan of Portsea Island,
1773

NAVAL ORDNANCE, H.M. GUNWHARF.

New Gunwharf: a response to a crisis

"We must destroy the English monarchy or expect to be destroyed by these intriguing and enterprising islanders - let us concentrate on the navy" Napoleon Bonaparte, 1797

Events in Europe, exacerbated by Napoleon's rise to power in the 1790s, generated a climate of fear throughout the country and led to an expansion of Britain's armed services and fortifications. The number of naval ships virtually doubled between 1780 and 1800. Between 1793 when the wars against France began, and the final defeat of Napoleon in 1815, government expenditure created a debt of £578 million. During an economic crisis of 1810-12, unemployment rose, food became scarce and discontent spread as the wars ground on devouring the country's resources.

The world's largest industrial complex

At Portsmouth's dockyard, after several years of planning, the Great Basin was enlarged and dry docks added from 1799 following the plans of Sir Samuel Bentham, Inspector-General of Naval Works. He initiated the use of steam engines, machine tools (including Marc Brunel's innovative block-making machinery) and the early use of iron in buildings. The royal dockyard at Portsmouth expanded to become the world's largest industrial complex.

A new gunwharf

A review in 1797, under Bentham, led to the Board of Ordnance commissioning further wharf space 'for the improvement and enlargement of the Ordnance Gunwharf' on the 'ouze' (mudflats) next to the existing gunwharf and to the south of the mill creek. Under the direction of Royal Engineer, John Evelegh, quay wall construction and infilling seems to have started immediately.

The site

The proposed wharf, 'planned' in accordance with 18th century principles, would be built out from the 'sea line' defensive wall and rampart (which protected and contained the town moat) over the ooze. The creek, with its important tidal mill (the King's Mill) supplying flour to the Navy, had to be maintained. This new wharf became known as New Gunwharf, whilst the existing wharf became Old Gunwharf; the combined wharves formed Portsmouth's fifth gunwharf.

Layout plan of buildings and gun beds, showing progress of New Gunwharf construction, John Evelegh, c1798

Red lines denote completed foundations and quay walls

Left: Napoleon Bonaparte
Right: part of the 'ouze' (now ooze) in Portsmouth harbour

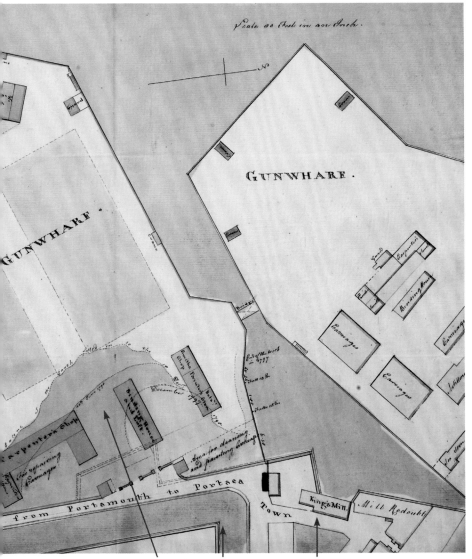

Progress of
wharf infill

Moat

King's Mill

Building New Gunwharf

	Building a gun wharf on ouze (to be built in low tide hours)
1	Build a Hard Way access across mud from shore for stone wagons, etc
2	Dig trench 4 feet deep and about 14 feet wide along planned line of quay
3	Hammer lines of 9x5 inch tongued and grooved Coffer Piles about 8 feet long into the mud/clay about 4 feet outside line of planned wharf edge
4	Lay 12x4 inch timber Sleeper on the bottom of the trench just behind the coffer wall and fix 9 inch square 11 feet long Ways (sleepers) on top across mud/clay every 3 feet
5	Nail a 12x10 inch Mud Sill (housed a couple of inches into the way) with a 6x9 inch Ribbon behind the top of the coffer and then 9x4 inch Planks to the end of the Ways, forming the quay wall foundation deck
6	Erect battered (raking) masonry quay wall on timber deck (with a projecting dowelled second course to take fenders) and backing brickwork and brickwork counterforts (buttressing)
7	Fit 12 inch square timber Fenders strapped at the top to long timber Land Ties running back from the quay wall
8	Finish quay wall with a timber Cap Sill and infill earth behind to sill level to form wharf, finishing with gravel

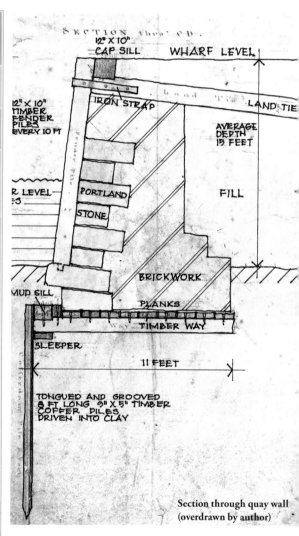

Section through quay wall
(overdrawn by author)

'PART of the FOUNDATIONS of the Commencemen of the WALL of the NEW GUN-WHARF John Evelegh Lt Colonel and Commanding Engineer, Portsmoutl Division, 4th April 1798'

Cofferdam Piles

Mud sill

Ribbon

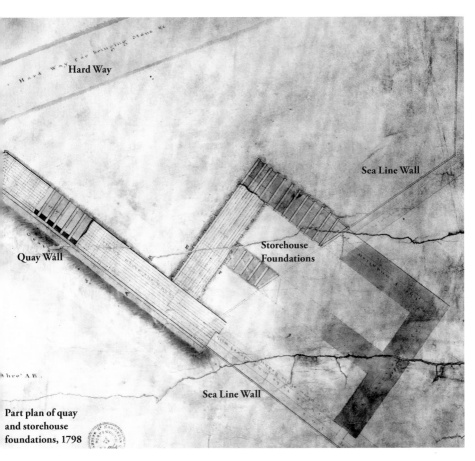

Hard Way

Sea Line Wall

Quay Wall

Storehouse
Foundations

Sea Line Wall

**Part plan of quay
and storehouse
foundations, 1798**

hese extracts show details of the quay wall onstruction. Once the timber-plank deck (5) as complete, the immensely heavy quay wall f limestone blocks and brickwork was built n top and anchored back with long land ties. nfill for the reclamation was brought from entham's new south dry docks and spread etween the quay walls to form the new site.

The plan shows the foundations for the first building, the Store for Unserviceable Stores, straddling the 17th century sea wall (pink) and redan. It is a mystery why it was planned at such a difficult location. Foundations on the seaward side (left) had to be deep down in the mud; on the other side the foundations were shallower resting on the old redan. These differing foundations and the solid stone wall could easily have split the building in two.

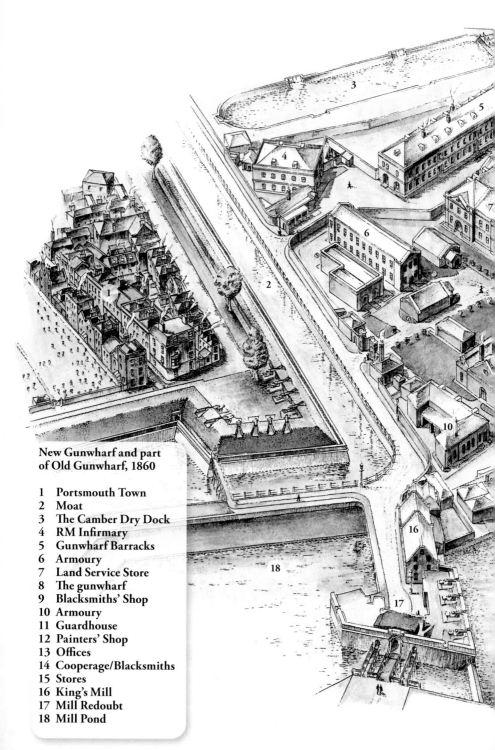

New Gunwharf and part of Old Gunwharf, 1860

1 Portsmouth Town
2 Moat
3 The Camber Dry Dock
4 RM Infirmary
5 Gunwharf Barracks
6 Armoury
7 Land Service Store
8 The gunwharf
9 Blacksmiths' Shop
10 Armoury
11 Guardhouse
12 Painters' Shop
13 Offices
14 Cooperage/Blacksmiths
15 Stores
16 King's Mill
17 Mill Redoubt
18 Mill Pond

H.M. Gunwharf Portsmouth c. 1860
© Robert Kennedy 2000

Store for Unserviceable Stores

Designed by Samuel Bentham's Royal Engineers as a store for defective munitions, this building has now been converted into apartments as Old Infirmary House

New Gunwharf was designed to work in tandem with the older wharf, the two areas being connected by a swing bridge; it was essentially one great gunwharf with extensive quaysides. The two most important initial buildings were the Store for Unserviceable Stores and the Sea Storehouse.

The wharf was organised into three zones:
1. the western munitions arrival/dispatch area with cranes and stores
2. the central gun-beds section, Sea Storehouse and guardhouse;
3. the eastern maintenance/repair shops with their Store for Unserviceable Stores;

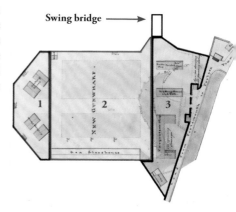

Swing bridge →

The three zones of New Gunwharf

Old Infirmary House

54

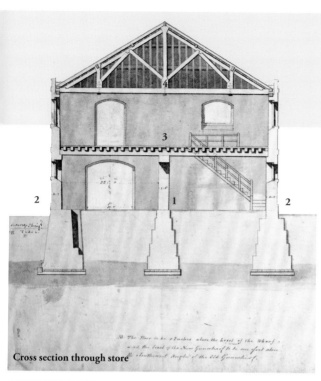

Cross section through store

1 Innovative 450mm central
  spine wall (columns or posts
  more usual)
2 675mm (2ft 3in) external walls
  designed to take heavy loads
3 First floor with 50mm (2in)
  floor boards on 175x190mm
  (7x7½in) joists at 375mm (15in)
  spacing on 300mm square
  (12in)beams
4 Substantial roof trusses (king
  and queen posts and secondary
  principal rafters, braced off
  the posts)

Never used for munitions

The Store for Unserviceable
Stores was used by the
Victualling Department from
its 1808 completion to 1824;
it then became the Royal
Marines Artillery Infirmary
for nearly 70 years. After the
Marines moved to Hilsea it
was converted to a schoolroom, library and married
soldiers quarters. In its 20th
century Vernon days, it was
a photographic studio and a
canteen.

Below: Arch to spine wall
foundation, excavated 1998

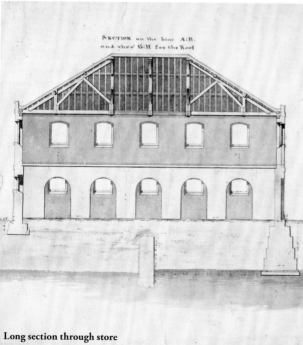

Long section through store

Sea Storehouse

Location

Foundations for the Sea Storehouse were built along the new quay wall and off the ooze as with the Store for Unserviceable Stores. The building was probably complete by 1810 but built approximately 30m (100ft) shorter than originally intended.

The construction of external brick walls and a central brick spine with large king and queen-post trusses to the roof was substantially the same as for the smaller store. Again this building was never used for its original purpose but, after its initial use as a victualling store, became the Royal Marines Artillery barracks.

Fire in 1935 largely destroyed the western half which was demolished and replaced; the eastern section was damaged by bombing six years later and itself replaced.

Right: **Lord Nelson died on board Victory at the Battle of Trafalgar in 1805. By then the building of New Gunwharf was well underway**

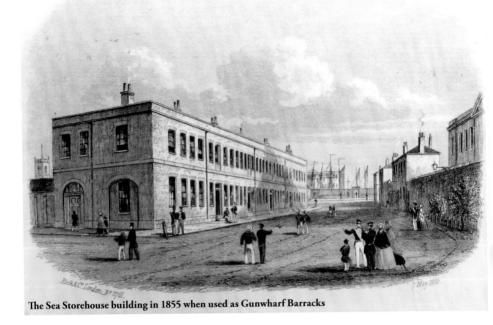

The Sea Storehouse building in 1855 when used as Gunwharf Barracks

Nelson Gate

This structure was completed about two years before Nelson's victory at Trafalgar

Location

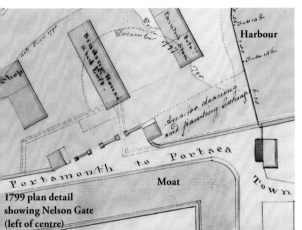

1799 plan detail
showing Nelson Gate
(left of centre)

Harbour

Moat

Portsmouth to Portsea Town

Nelson Gate was the main entrance through the boundary wall into New Gunwharf from the Portsmouth to dockyard road. The gateway with its attendant guards' lodges was probably complete by 1802. It followed the standard dockyard pattern of a central vehicle gateway with flanking pedestrian doorways. To mark the gate's importance, its principal piers were surmounted by Portland stone mortars. The structure was restored in 1999.

Nelson Gate
today

Storekeeper's Offices

This early purpose-built office block is now the Old Customs House pub at Gunwharf Quays

Now that another wharf had been added, the officers' quarters and offices had become remote from the business of the much larger complex. A new storekeeper's offices building was constructed on the southern edge of Old Gunwharf, facing the bridge connecting both wharves. Officers and clerks now had an excellent view of their valuable guns and stores, and the loading and off-loading operations from hoys and wherries.

For its modest size this is a grand building in a classical style with an elegant central pediment; it was also well-planned for its purpose. The Flemish brickwork has alternating red stretchers and dark kiln-burnt headers, typical of the new buildings at Gunwharf.

Looking across to the Grand Storehouse (Vulcan) and quays from inside the Old Customs House pub (Storekeeper's Offices), c1811

Section to the left and plans below show the offices - most with a fireplace. There were individual presses (wardrobes) for senior staff (ground floor), and a communal one for junior staff (first floor). English Heritage insisted that the room layout remained.

Left: Press used to store clothes or linen (see plans)

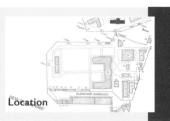

Location

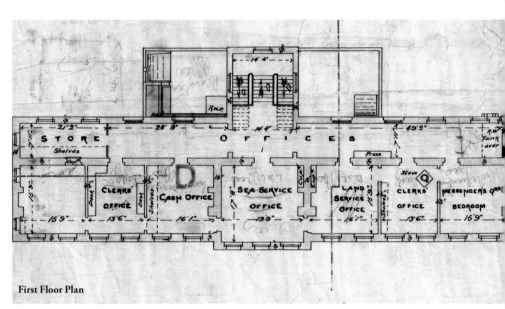

First Floor Plan

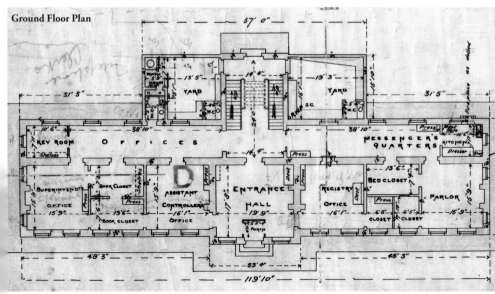

Ground Floor Plan

A victualling wharf and the Long Storehouse

A new order was issued: 'the two storehouses are to be transferred to the Victualling Department'

A new victualling wharf

Portsmouth town had been the focus for food supply for the armed services since the time of Henry VIII. Its main victualling quay, hard pressed for space, was adjacent to the new gun wharf with its storehouses; it was too good an opportunity to miss. A revised plan for Gunwharf was agreed around 1810 allocating a quarter of the new wharf and its storehouses for victualling.

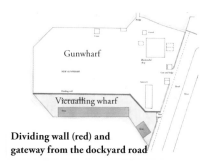

Dividing wall (red) and gateway from the dockyard road

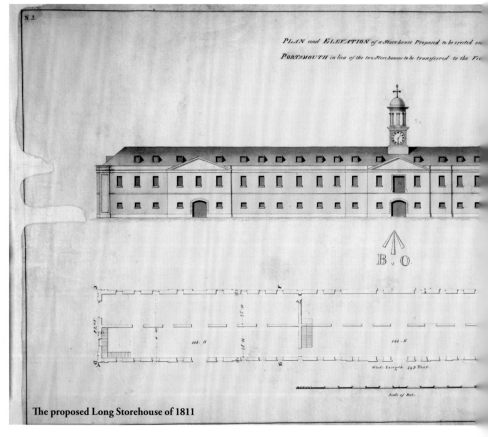

The proposed Long Storehouse of 1811

Location

Royal Engineer John Evelegh was commanded to draw up plans for a replacement ordnance store equal in area to the two relinquished stores. It was to face north over the gun beds, just like the Sea Storehouse.

The Long Storehouse

This would have been the second longest ordnance storehouse in Britain after the Grand Storehouse in Old Gunwharf. It was in effect three storehouses in one great building. Each storehouse section had a central projecting section and a triangular pediment. A tall clock tower crowned the central section. All doorways were in the north and end elevations.

The superstructure was designed on a grand scale with much higher interiors than the earlier storehouses and a well-supported attic providing additional storage space. Its ground floor had a brick spine wall as before. But the Long Storehouse was never built.

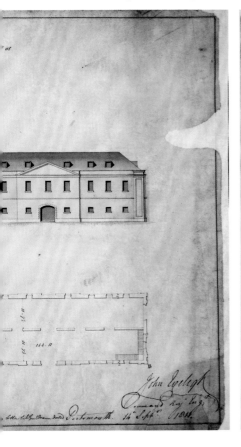

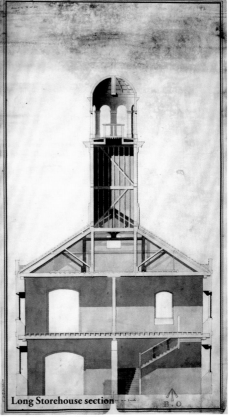

Long Storehouse section

Designing the Grand Storehouse

*Facing the harbour it would impress all
approaching by land and sea*

A decision was made that a building as splendid as the Long Storehouse should face towards the harbour. As the Long Storehouse design was too long to fit across the site, it was abandoned. Evelegh and his team then brilliantly transformed the original plan by turning both end sections through 90 degrees to form 'wings' that would reach out towards the harbour entrance creating three sides of a quadrangle. All that was needed was a slight adjustment to the victualling department wall. There was now a grand pedimented elevation looking west to the harbour, east to the town, north across to the Storekeeper's offices, and southwards, lording it over the victualling stores.

Another outcome of these changes was that the quality of the architecture was significantly enhanced. The proportions of the pedimented sections were improved and the central section was given an additional half-storey (called

an attic storey). Doorways now had half-round rather than segmental arches and the main entrances were given elegant stonework surrounds and columns. The clock tower was enriched with paired corner columns and well proportioned arches. All this resulted in a fine piece of architecture; Evelegh and his team were as much architects as they were engineers.

A commemorative stone above the east central arch records the date 1814 and the name of Benjamin Fisher, promoted to succeed Evelegh. He had a major part in the construction of this building and may have been responsible for the quadrangle concept and the design refinements.

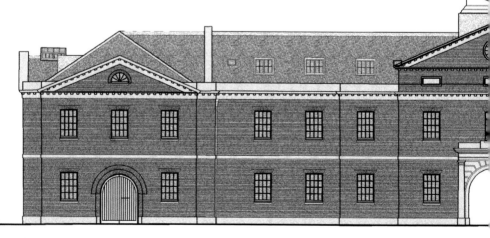

Clock tower

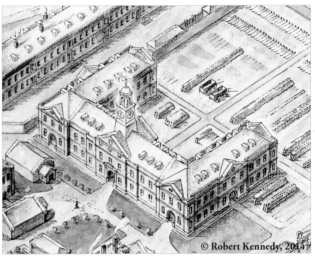

Above: Grand Storehouse
Left: Commemorative Stone (above cornice) -
inscription partially eroded. East entrance
Below: Grand Storehouse - east elevation
(drawing - HGP Architects, 1999)

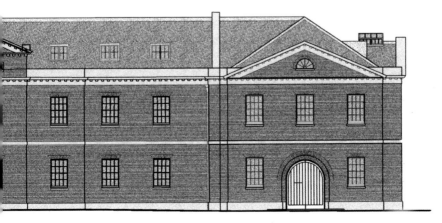

Constructing the Grand Storehouse

Building started on the Grand Storehouse in the autumn of 1811 following the form of construction agreed for the Long Storehouse project

The substructure or foundations

Two options for the foundations had been prepared (see below). The cheaper option was chosen, although deeper foundations were used adjacent to two pairs of underground vaults designed to collect rain water from the gutters for fire-fighting.

The superstructure - built to store heavy loads

Ground floor accommodation

The height is 4.8m (16ft). The first floor rests on the solid brick external walls and a central spine wall, which stops short of all lateral external walls with bull-nosed stone blocks. There are sliding sash windows (taller than shown on the section). The floor was of stone block paving.

First floor accommodation

This has a height to the underside of beams of 4.1m (13ft 9in). The floor construction with 50mm (2in) floor boards on joists sitting on 300mm (1ft) square timber beams, sits on wall plates within 780mm (2ft 7in) brick walls. Central timber posts assist the support of the attic floor. There are tall sliding sash windows.

Top floor accommodation

The attic was constructed with strong timber roof trusses with twin posts allowing central access to a storage floor. They sit on timber bearers called wall plates on the external walls. The attic is lit by dormer windows. Lead-lined gutters lie behind brick parapet walls.

OPTION 1: DEEP BRICK FOUNDATIONS	
1	Excavate fill down to the clay of the former harbour bed
2	Drive 3m (10ft) timber piles into the clay; construct a timber deck of planks on top
3	Build 6m (20ft) high stepped foundation walls off the deck
4	Back-fill the excavated material to wharf level
NB	This was the most expensive option but the location of the piles in the clay would ensure their durability

OPTION 2: SHALLOW BRICK FOUNDATIONS	
1	Excavate fill to depth of only 1.5m (5ft)
2	Drive 6m (20ft) timber piles into the clay; construct a timber deck of planks on top
3	Build 1.5m (5ft) high stepped foundation walls off the deck
4	Back-fill the excavated material to wharf level
NB	This, with its limited excavation and shallow brickwork, was the most economical, but Evelegh had concern about durability of the piles

The deep stepped brick foundations (shown immediately to the right) formed the best solution for a stable foundation to this large storehouse. However, the lower cost, timber piled, solution (on the opposite page) was used.

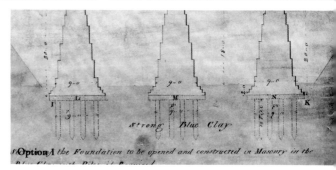

Shoes, candleholder and gun elevation holder found in Storehouse vaults (*right*)

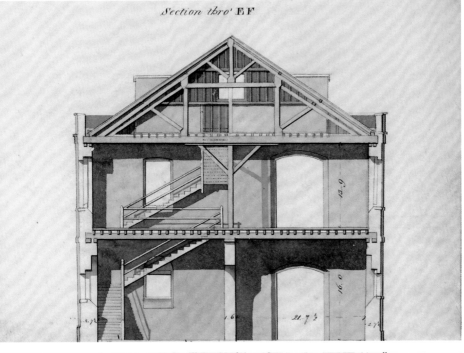

Section thro' EF

13.9

16.0

2.7½   1.6   21.7½   2.7½

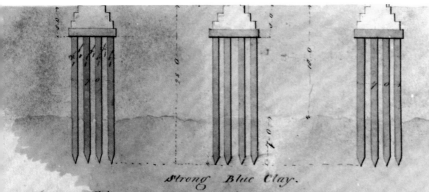

25.0

18.0

Strong Blue Clay.

Section shewing the Piles driven within 5 Feet of the
Surface, which is considered objectionable as the

16   Red.
in an Inch.
Option 2

The Grand Storehouse

The grandest storehouse of British ordnance yards has been restored and converted into apartments, restaurant and an art gallery

The Grand Storehouse, known as Vulcan since the days of HMS Vernon, was the largest ordnance storehouse attached to a dockyard in Britain before 1900 and one of the larger naval storehouses of any type. It was described by local historian, Dr Henry Slight in 1820 as a "..stupendous building which might vie with the proudest boast of Italy!".

Building began on the quadrangular storehouse in 1811. In November that year a crowd of "respectable inhabitants of the town and neighbourhood", military officers, "ladies and persons of distinction", gathered to see the Duke of Clarence lay a bed of mortar on the foundations for a special block of Portland stone.

This storehouse took three years to complete but was in service as an artillery store for more than a hundred. Within its walls were stored cannon, gun carriages and other stores, including shot, swords, rifles, other small arms, gunflints, boarding hooks, tools, shell holders, and much more.

Looking up *at the hatchway in Vulcan's central passageway*

1811
WAS THE YEAR
Jane Austen published her first novel, *Sense and Sensibility*

The building was well arrange with hatches centrally in eac section and at the souther end of both wings. It wa accessed by wide double door in the external walls. Pulley were arranged at attic leve so stores could be taken to or removed from, all area

The Duke of Clarence (1765-1837)
For a brief time Lord High Admiral, later King William IV (the 'Sailor King'). During his reign, in 1833, slavery was abolished throughout the British empire

Flemish bond - *alternate stretchers and headers*

English bond - *alternative rows of stretchers and header*

The brickwork was arranged in Flemish brick bond with alternating red stretcher bricks and blue/black, sometimes glazed, burnt header bricks. These headers are produced by high temperatures and the potash coming from wood-fuelled firing; they often have a good black glaze. The overall effect is a soft grey patterning to the red brickwork; in sunlight the glazed headers sparkle attractively.

The Grand Storehouse (Vulcan) from the west

Penny-struck lime mortar joints - *joints formed using penny and ruler in high-quality brickwork*

The internal surfaces - walls, timber beams, joists and floorboards - were coated with limewash. This is a method of painting walls with coats of dilute lime putty (obtained from the burning of lime and its slaking with water). It can have a cleansing and disinfecting effect.

Gunwharf: 1815 to 1850

By 1815 Portsmouth's gunwharf had become the biggest ever built in Britain

Opposite left to right: Shell magazine, Royal Clarence Yard, King's Mill

Old Gunwharf contained officers' quarters, administration offices, large storehouses and a huge new painters' shop; New Gunwharf was now the main gun storage area with its Grand Storehouse as well as its munitions maintenance department. This period saw further building works including a second armoury and three shell magazines.

Gunwharf and the Grand Storehouse from the east side of the mill pond. The mill is the small building in the centre

Gunwharf Barracks

From the late 17th century and throughout the 18th century a victualling establishment, known as Weovil's (later Weevil's) Yard, emerged across the harbour at Gosport and, by 1824, the victualling wharf at Gunwharf was free to be used for other purposes. By 1832 the premises at Gosport had developed into a large purpose-built victualling department, Royal Clarence Yard.

The Royal Marines Artillery immediately took over the vacated victualling wharf at Gunwharf to ensure proper security. The larger storehouse became quarters for officers and soldiers and the smaller store became an infirmary. A canteen, a cell-block and even a women's washhouse were built against the dividing wall. The RMA were to remain at Gunwharf for the next 34 years, followed by the Army Ordnance Corps until 1891.

King's Mill

Between the two wharves on the landward side was the King's Mill. Established in early medieval times, this tidal mill was substantially rebuilt after 1574 by Thomas Beeston when he added a mill house and an improved bridge across the creek, which ran from the large inland mill pond. In the early 18th century the Beeston family sold the mill to the Crown. From this time it was known as King's Mill. It was integrated into Bernard de Gomme's late 17th century fortification of Portsmouth, with the addition of the Mill Redoubt.

By the 1780s it comprised a large tidal mill with twin water-wheels, a storehouse, two flour drying ovens and a substantial mill house. The mill burnt down in 1868 and soon after, work began on re-filling the now redundant mill pond, part of which was added to Gunwharf.

OLD GUNWHARF

. Lodge
. Watch House
. Engine House
. Gun Carriage Store
. ditto
. ditto
. ditto
. Sea Service Store
. Stores
0. ditto
1. Office
2. Painters Shop
3. Store
4. Office
5. Painters Shop
6. Cart Shed
7. Cooperage
8. Blacksmiths Shop
9. Engine Room
0. Gun Shed

21. Gun Carriage Store
22. ditto
23. ditto
24. Sea Service Store
25. Smithy
26. North Store
27. Stables
28. Coach House
29. Deputy Storekeepers Qrs
30. 1st Class Clerks Qrs
31. 2nd Class Clerks Qrs
32. 1st Class Clerks Qrs
33. Storekeepers Qrs
34. Armoury
35. Stables
36. Lodge

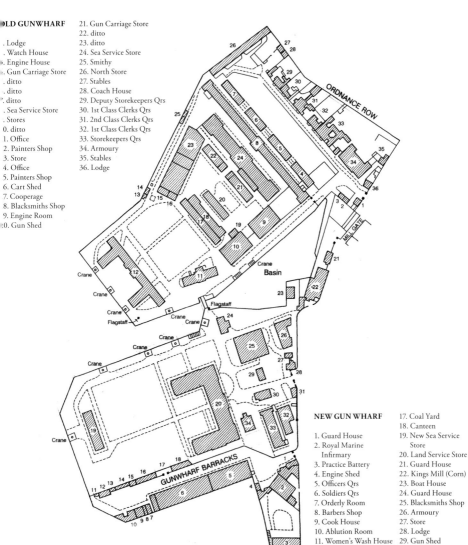

NEW GUN WHARF

1. Guard House
2. Royal Marine Infirmary
3. Practice Battery
4. Engine Shed
5. Officers Qrs
6. Soldiers Qrs
7. Orderly Room
8. Barbers Shop
9. Cook House
10. Ablution Room
11. Women's Wash House
12. Serjeants Mess
13. Cook House
14. Stores
15. Bk. Serjeants Qrs
16. Regimental Cells

17. Coal Yard
18. Canteen
19. New Sea Service Store
20. Land Service Store
21. Guard House
22. Kings Mill (Corn)
23. Boat House
24. Guard House
25. Blacksmiths Shop
26. Armoury
27. Store
28. Lodge
29. Gun Shed
30. Shell Magazine
31. Store
32. Shell Magazine
33. Armoury
34. Shell Magazine

Plan of Gunwharf, Portsmouth, 1859

Steam, iron and shells

Advanced steam-power and the railways introduced a new phase of the Industrial Revolution bringing wealth and prosperity to the country

La Gloire

After the Crimean War (1853-1856) Britain enjoyed a period of relative peace. However, although Britain and France had been allies during the war, their relationship was never close, particularly as France, encouraged by the victory over Russia, sought to extend her influence in Europe. Fears that the French might consider an invasion of Britain were exacerbated when France launched the world's first iron clad ship (with steam power), *La Gloire*, in 1859. Navies around the world responded as wooden warships became redundant overnight. Britain built her own steam-powered iron-clad warships: *Warrior* in 1860 and *Black Prince* in 1861.

German ambitions and the War Office

Later on, fears about a threat from France were replaced by concerns over German ambitions, especially under Kaiser Wilhelm, generating an arms race towards the end of the 19th century.

The Board of Ordnance was abolished in 1855 and its functions were incorporated into the War Office. This led to far-reaching changes including, at Gunwharf, the Army Ordnance Corps replacing the Marines at the barracks.

Gunwharf now had the responsibility for ensuring the new British iron-clad warships were properly armed; bigger guns and explosive shells designed to pierce metal-clad enemy warships had evolved. At the same time new powerful families of weapons - mines and torpedoes - were emerging. Workshop facilities (for the service and repair of stores) at Gunwharf were up-graded; the blacksmith's shop was extended and in due course became the Royal Ordnance Factories.

Gunwharf extension and the railway

Anxieties about an assault from longer range guns led to the construction of a ring of massive forts (known as Palmerston's Follies) from Fort Gilkicker, west of Gosport, to Fort Cumberland, east of Southsea, to protect Portsmouth from land and sea. The town fortifications became redundant and in the 1870s were demolished, releasing land for new developments.

Around the same time plans were also being made to fill in the mill pond. These

New Gunwharf's wall and gates, 1876-78

Southern end, with guérite (stone sentry pulpit)

Old South Gate

Old Central Gate

1851

WAS THE YEAR of the Great Exhibition in London, opened by Queen Victoria

HMS *Warrior*, 1860

The harbour extension railway today

changes made possible a railway extension from the centre of Portsmouth to the harbour by The Joint Portsmouth Extension Railway Company. Work creating the necessary embankments and bridges began around 1873. The railway ran along the old north bank of the mill pond and curved towards the harbour taking a slice of the east end of Gunwharf. By 1876 the railway was complete.

The in-filling of the mill pond (and the town moat) made possible a considerable eastern extension to Gunwharf with new high enclosing walls and gateways. The old dockyard road was rebuilt around the outside. In compensation for the loss of land at the east end of Gunwharf, the railway company built houses on the new land for the Commissary General and his deputy, and other buildings.

Wall built to accommodate mill pond levels

Main Gate

NEW GUN WHARF
PORTSMOUTH

Zincographed and Printed at the School of Military Engineering, Chatham,
under the direction of Capt. R.H.Bill, R.E.
Major General ___ Hewett C.M.G., R.E. Commandant.

Litho showing ___ ___
___ some time prior ___
1892.

1876-1878 GUNWHARF WALL

OLD PORTSMOUTH AND TOWN WALL

CHURCH YARD
(disused)

AREA TAKEN FROM RAMPARTS AND MOAT

MILL POND INFILLED

AREA TAKEN FROM PORTSEA

MILL REDOUBT

OLD GATES

Armoury.

OLD GUN WHARF

BASIN

Guns and turrets

The period 1850 to 1915 saw developments in shells, replacing shot; in the power and size of naval guns; and in steam and then steam-turbine engines, replacing sails.

This led to armoured, mast-less, iron-hulled warships with heavy guns fitted permanently onto ships in rotating turrets. HMS *Devastation* (1871) was the first and HMS *Dreadnought* (1906) the most revolutionary of these early battleships.

The need for gun storage and gunwharves diminished correspondingly during this period.

| | Total | | 1 | 7 | 1 | 300 | | 2 | | 1:250 |

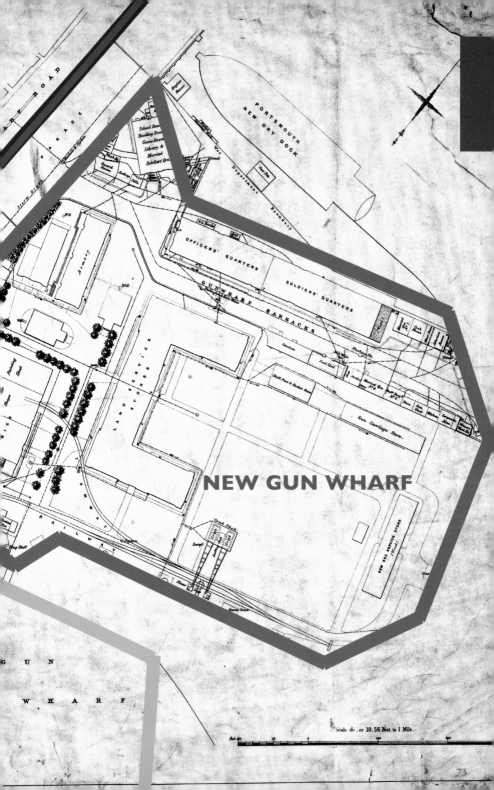

PORTSMOUTH
NEW DRY DOCK

OFFICERS' QUARTERS

SOLDIERS' QUARTERS

GUNWHARF BARRACKS

NEW GUN WHARF

RAILWAY

GUN WHARF

Scale 5b. or 10.56 Feet to 1 Mile.

73

Gunwharf divided: 1889-1918

Commanding Officer's house, 1901

Quartermaster's house, 1901   C.O.stables, 1901

For some years the Royal Navy had followed a policy known as 'the two nation standard' whereby Britain must have at least as many battleships as the next two largest navies combined. This strategy did not seem too extravagant for what had become the British Empire - the largest empire the world had ever seen. The policy was formalised by the Naval Defence Act of 1889 and resulted in the commissioning of 71 new warships. Major expansion in support services was required, heralding a significant period of building construction at Gunwharf.

Another factor affecting Gunwharf at this time was a dispute between the War Office and the Admiralty resulting in the division of the site into New Gunwharf for the navy and Old Gunwharf for the army. By 1891 each half had its own commanding ordnance officer.

A new century

The start of the 20th century was a period of massive change. In addition to the increasing demand for high calibre guns and the on-going development of underwater warfare there was a revolution in naval power - the development of Dreadnought battleships. The steam turbine engine gave unprecedented speed to this latest type of warship which relied entirely on large guns. Dreadnoughts reignited the arms race.

During the 1914-18 World War the Portsmouth Division depots - Gunwharf, Priddy's Hard, Tipner, Marchwood, and especially New Gunwharf - were kept fully employed in maintaining vast supplies of ammunition to the Royal Navy.

Military Gunwharf North

New stores, 1889

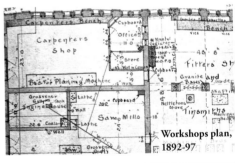

Workshops plan, 1892-97

Workshops elevation, 1896-7

Commissary General's house, 1881

Commissary General's house, 1881

Commissary General's house

Deputy C.G. house, 1881

Deputy C.G. house, 1881

C.G. stables, 1881

Naval Gunwharf South

Royal Ordnance Factories

The workshop complex on the naval side developed from the Blacksmiths' Shop (c1810) into the Royal Ordnance Factories. It had an important workshop role for HMS Vernon until 1945 completing a history of nearly 150 years.

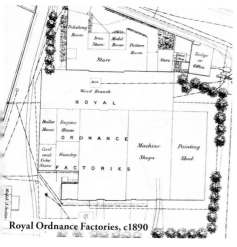

Royal Ordnance Factories, c1890

Workshops, 1902

Shell/fuse store, 1876

Carriage store, 1877

Armourer's shop, 1899

Royal Engineers Record Plan, 1916

Gunwharf dispersed: 1916-1920

In 1872 a school had been established in Portsmouth Harbour for torpedo trails and training. For fifty years this establishment, named HMS Vernon, occupied an assembly of redundant ships known as hulks. But by the First World War torpedoes (and mines) had become too important and the hulks too decrepit for this situation to continue.

From as early as 1908 many thought Vernon should be brought ashore. But it took ten years to agree on a location and approve a budget (£742,000). Gunwharf was chosen: it was to be united once more and handed to the Admiralty. The War Department retained a military gunwharf, shown in red on the 1914-16 plan (left), at Gunwharf but all stores and accommodation were transferred to Hilsea. The Naval Ordnance Department crossed the harbour to new premises (completed by 1920) just north of Priddy's Hard Armaments Depot. These two dispersed gunwharves formed the sixth and final gunwharf establishment in Portsmouth.

The most urgent need had been for self-contained accommodation for the Mining Branch (including its new experimental mining design section) and it came ashore in advance of the rest of Vernon in 1916. The Land Service Stores (Vulcan) on the southern site and other adjacent buildings, including two large recently built sheds, became its new home. The remaining departments came ashore from 1919.

The work of the ordnance wharves continues today at Defence Munitions at Gosport and elsewhere.

Fitter's shop, Naval Gunwharf

Priddy's Hard and Gunwharf, Gosport

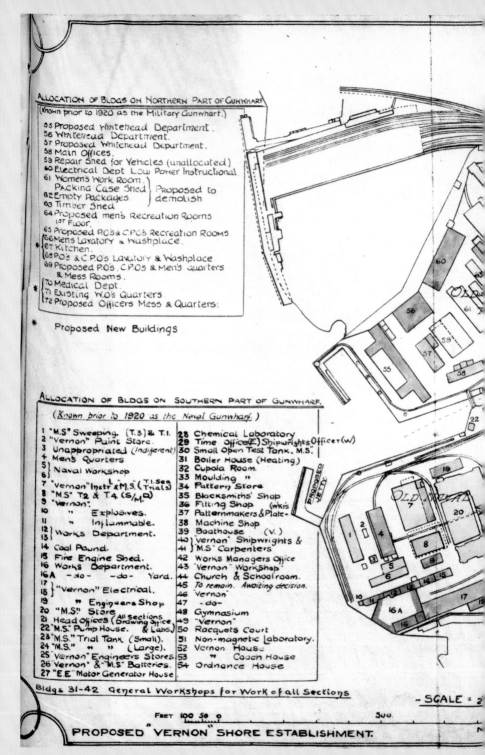

ALLOCATION OF BLDGS ON NORTHERN PART OF GUNWHARF.

(Known prior to 1920 as the Military Gunwharf.)

55 Proposed Whitehead Department.
56 Whitehead Department.
57 Proposed Whitehead Department.
58 Main Offices.
59 Repair Shed for Vehicles (unallocated)
60 Electrical Dept Low Power Instructional.
61 Women's Work Room.
   Packing Case Shed ⎫ Proposed to
62 Empty Packages.   ⎬ demolish
63 Timber Shed   ⎭
64 Proposed men's Recreation Rooms
   1st Floor.
65 Proposed P.O's & C.P.O's Recreation Rooms.
66 Men's Lavatory & Washplace.
67 Kitchen.
68 P.O's & C.P.O's Lavatory & Washplace
69 Proposed P.O's, C.P.O's & Men's Quarters
   & Mess Rooms.
70 Medical Dept.
71 Existing W.O's Quarters.
72 Proposed Officers Mess & Quarters:

* Proposed New Buildings

ALLOCATION OF BLDGS ON SOUTHERN PART OF GUNWHARF.

(Known prior to 1920 as the Naval Gunwharf.)

1 "M.S" Sweeping. (T.3) & T.I.
2 "Vernon" Paint Store.
3 Unappropriated (Indifferent)
4 Men's Quarters
5 ⎫
6 ⎬ Naval Workshop
7 "Vernon" Instr & M.S. (T.I. Sea Trials)
8 "M.S" T2 & T4 (S/M Q)
9 "Vernon"
10 " Explosives.
11 " Inflammable.
12 ⎫ Works Department.
13 ⎭
14 Coal Pound.
15 Fire Engine Shed.
16 Works Department.
16A -do- -do- Yard.
17 ⎫
18 ⎬ "Vernon" Electrical.
19 " Engineers Shop
20 "M.S" Store
21 Head Offices (All Sections)
22 "M.S" Pump House. (Drawing Office & Labs.)
23 "M.S" Trial Tank (Small).
24 "M.S" " " (Large).
25 "Vernon" Engineers Stores
26 "Vernon" & "M.S" Batteries.
27 "E.E" Motor Generator House

28 Chemical Laboratory
29 Time Office(E) Shipwrights Officer(W)
30 Small Open Test Tank. M.S.
31 Boiler House (Heating)
32 Cupola Room.
33 Moulding "
34 Pattern Store
35 Blacksmiths' Shop
36 Fitting Shop (Wkrs
37 Patternmakers & Plate-
38 Machine Shop
39 Boathouse (V.)
40 ⎫ "Vernon" Shipwrights &
41 ⎬ "M.S" Carpenters
42 Works Managers Office
43 "Vernon" Workshop
44 Church & Schoolroom.
45 To remain. Awaiting decision.
46 "Vernon"
47 -do-
48 Gymnasium
49 "Vernon"
50 Racquets Court
51 Non-magnetic Laboratory.
52 Vernon House
53 " Coach House
54 Ordnance House

Bldgs 31-42 General Workshops for Work of all Sections

FEET 100 50 0   500.

~ SCALE = 2

PROPOSED "VERNON" SHORE ESTABLISHMENT.

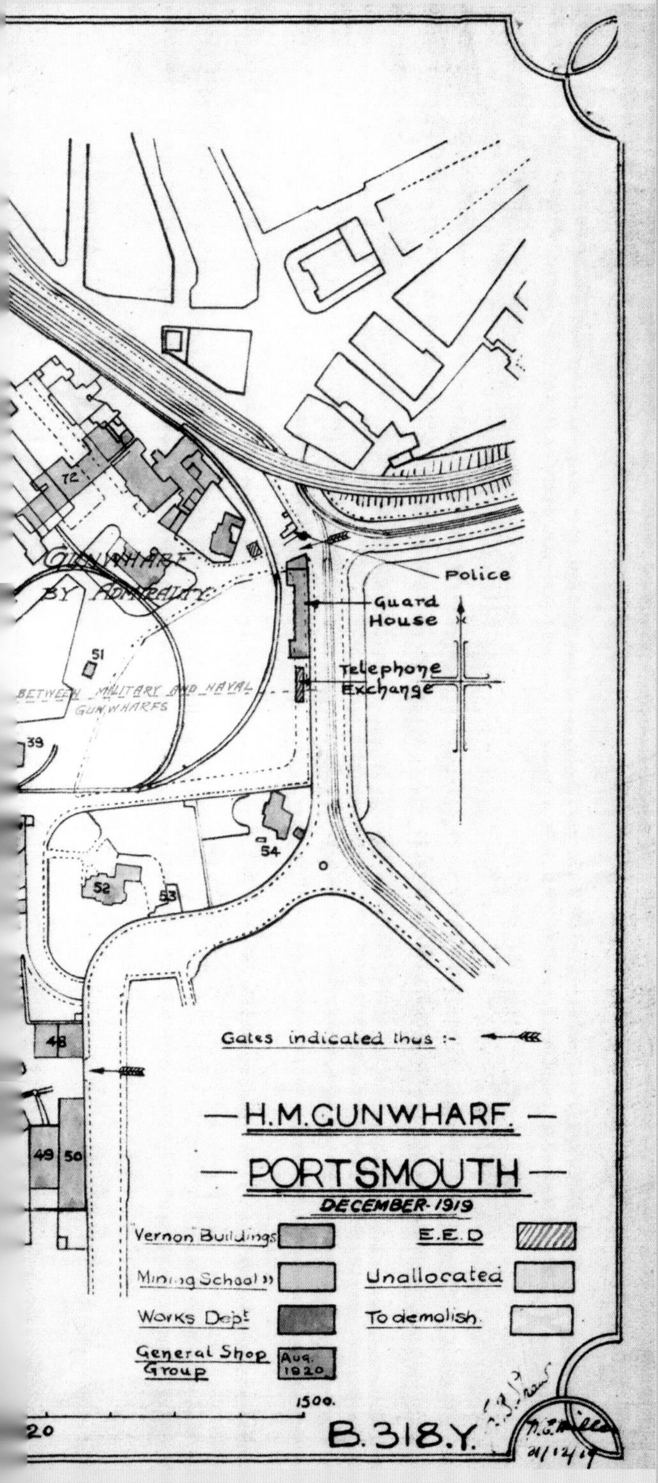
GUNWHARF
BY ADMIRALTY
72
51
BETWEEN MILITARY AND NAVAL
GUNWHARFS
39
Police
Guard House
Telephone Exchange
54
52
53
48
49
50
Gates indicated thus :-
— H.M.GUNWHARF. —
— PORTSMOUTH —
DECEMBER-1919
"Vernon" Buildings
E.E.D
Mining School "
Unallocated
Works Dept
To demolish.
General Shop Group
Aug. 1920
1500.
20
B.318.Y.

4

HMS VERNON

Torpedoes and mines

All underwater explosive devices including mines were known originally as 'torpedoes', a term first used by an American inventor, David Bushnell

Torpedoes

The first self-propelled device (now called a torpedo) was invented by Robert Whitehead, an English engineer working in Austria from 1856. Frequently modified, Whitehead torpedoes became the standard design into the 20th century.

Tubular weapons, made from steel, with a warhead, propulsion engine (electric from the late 19th century) and twin counter-rotating propellers, torpedoes were initially launched from underwater tubes in torpedo boats.

Magnetic Mine

Manufactured from 1871 under licence at the Royal Armoury, Woolwich, the torpedoes were stored and repaired in depots at Chatham, Portsmouth and Plymouth. Horsea Island in Portsmouth Harbour was used for testing from 1888.

Counter-measures had to be developed. Torpedo boat 'destroyers', used from the 1890s to attack enemy torpedo boats, developed into the modern class of warships known as destroyers, with combined hunting and torpedo-launching facilities. Torpedoes can be launched from many platforms including submarines, ships, helicopters and aircraft

and were widely used in both world wars. The first British naval submarine, Holland 1, is displayed at the Royal Navy Submarine Museum, Gosport.

Naval Mines

Despite only coming into significant use from the late 19th century, naval mines have a much longer history. Modern mines operate by contact (passing vessels striking 'horns' on the mine), by shore operation, or by influence (variations in magnetic fields caused by ships, acoustic detection or water pressure changes). There are moored mines, bottom or ground (sea-bed) mines, limpet mines (attached to ships' hulls) and mobile mines (propelled to a planned location). Produced in many shapes and sizes, the most common mines have spherical cases, made of steel, aluminium, or even glass-reinforced fibre.

Again counter-measures had to be devised, as well as methods of mine-sweeping (location and destruction), mine-hunting, and clearance diving (manual deactivation).

Huge numbers of these deadly weapons were used in both world wars. Extensive mine clearance took place after the Second World War but many still remain.

Torpedo

HMS Vernon afloat

Left: Admiral of the Fleet, Lord 'Jacky' Fisher
Right: Sir Henry Jackson, FRS

HMS Vernon, a new section of the floating establishment HMS Excellent Gunnery School, was formed in 1872, under Commander 'Jacky' Fisher, for the study of torpedo warfare and electrical technology on ships. It was named after the first old hulk that was added to Excellent to provide its accommodation.

After its independence from Excellent in 1876, other hulks, such as *Ariadne, Florence Nightingale* and later, *Actaeon, Donegal* and others, were added to Vernon in a series of complex adaptations.

Originally moored near the dockyard, the Vernon establishment was later moved to Portchester Creek. Other important hulks to join included the *Marlborough* and then in 1904 the redundant 1861 iron-clad warship HMS *Warrior*.

As well as work on electrical systems for gun firing, the use of dynamos and searchlights, lighting systems, electric motors, and developments in the use of radio were part of the later work of the floating Vernon.

1875
WAS THE YEAR
Alexander Graham Bell, inventor of the telephone, visited Vernon

The technically brilliant Lieutenant Henry Jackson was at Vernon for over three years from 1881 and then, when Captain, carried out work with Guglielmo Marconi, the well known pioneer in wireless telegraphy. Jackson returned later to Vernon to supervise the installation of the first wireless sets in ships. He was an important early scientist in the Vernon story, one of a long and distinguished line, eventually becoming Admiral of the Fleet.

The Portsmouth Torpedo School, permanently retaining the name HMS Vernon, developed into a vital training and experimental centre for torpedo and mine warfare, and for electrical technology and equipment. Such was the importance of Vernon that Queen Victoria visited the establishment in 1889.

Vernon hulks in Portchester Creek

HMS Vernon comes ashore

On 1st October 1923 the pennant of the Captain of HMS Vernon was hoisted at Gunwharf, marking the beginning of a new shore establishment

Even before 1914 it was recognised that the line of hulks forming the HMS Vernon enterprise in Portchester Creek was inadequate. Well-equipped laboratories were essential as was better accommodation and sanitation. The Gunwharf, where the Mining School had relocated from 1916, was an obvious choice and in 1919 it was decided to move the entire Vernon establishment ashore.

The site was extensively re-developed and carefully planned (the title page of this section shows an early proposal). New purpose-built accommodation was built, mainly on the northern side, where around twenty buildings were demolished and others were substantially rebuilt. This involved the removal of some historically important buildings such as the 1720 Grand Storehouse, officers' quarters, entrance gateways, and the impressive 1797 Armoury.

Buildings were named after the historic hulks and ships that had served the 'floating' Vernon for nearly fifty years. By 1920 the War Department had moved out of Old Gunwharf and building work had begun.

This was to be a new phase for both Gunwharf and the work of HMS Vernon. The Mining, Torpedo and Electrical departments were re-formed, each supervised by a Commander. The Admiralty's 1919 Mine Design Department (MDD), a section of the Admiralty Experimental Station, was also to be part of the new HMS Vernon.

Residential

The residential areas of the new HMS Vernon were laid out like a village around a large green. Ariadne, the new officers' building (Wardroom), with its accommodation wings, pediment and Tuscan style portico looked over gardens from the north. Its architecture was in a 'wrenaissance' style (popular from about 1890 to the 1920s) with stone quoins (corner blocks) in brick facades, well-proportioned classical sliding sash windows, corniced eaves, and tiled roofs. The building group with its two angled linked wings, one on either side, followed 'butterfly' plan idea fashionable during the Edwardian period. The new Defiance and Nightingale buildings were in a similar style.

Excellent sports facilities were provided with squash courts, a gymnasium, and a central football and sports field (built over the site of the King's Mill). Tennis courts were dotted around the site for the various ranks.

Industrial

The industrial areas were sited closer to the harbour and used both converted and purpose built buildings.

Ariadne Wardroom (left) and front lawn, photo, 1932

Instruction Room, 1930s

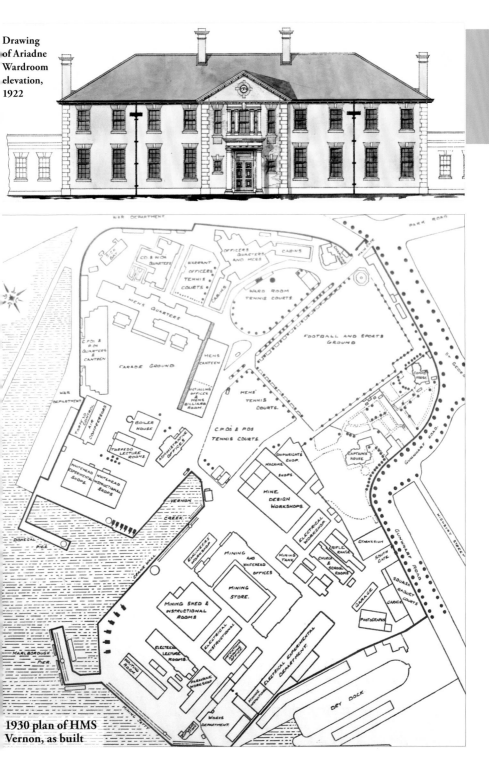

Drawing of Ariadne Wardroom elevation, 1922

1930 plan of HMS Vernon, as built

The Battle of Mines

The work of HMS Vernon continued during the inter-war years with the development of Motor Torpedo Boats (MTBs) being an important new feature.

War is declared

Immediately following British Prime Minister Neville Chamberlain's declaration of war on Germany in September 1939, the Germans, who were well-prepared, began laying mines off the east coast of England. On 16 September a 10,000 ton passenger ship, City of Paris, struck one of these mines and had to be towed into the Thames, damaged and with one crew member dead. Two days later Winston Churchill, First Lord of the Admiralty, came down to Vernon to discuss this early threat with the Mining School and Mine Design Department (MDD).

HMS Vulcan with first MTB flotilla alongside

The race to discover mines

The Mining School and MDD were particularl[y] busy in the first six months of the war and carried out vital work for the defence of th[e] nation. Dr Albert Wood, Chief Scientist o[f] MDD from October 1939, led an initially sma[ll] team of less than 25 scientists and technicians.

At the start of the war the British did no[t] have any intelligence on the new magneti[c] mines used by the Germans. Minesweeping, a procedure used by ships to clear mines b[y] detonation, confirmed that the enemy wa[s] using these mines but could produce n[o] information about them. So the race was on t[o] retrieve undetonated German mines in order t[o] examine them and discover their secrets.

The Shoeburyness mines

On 23 November 1939 a German parachut[e] mine was located off Shoeburyness at th[e] mouth of the Thames estuary. After initia[l] deactivation, the mine was stored overnigh[t] at a police lodge before being brought t[o] Vernon where it was placed in a laborator[y] behind sentry-guarded doors. Wood, with tw[o] other scientists and two naval men, carefull[y] examined the mine which turned out to be [a] magnetic type. A second, much larger mine wa[s]

Churchill's visit to HMS Vernon, September 21, 1939

Right: Mining tank at Vernon
Far right: HMS Vernon badge
Left: Defusing a mine at Brighton
Far left: WWII Mine at Gunwharf Quays

recovered later that day. This pattern would be repeated many times over subsequent years. The danger these and other men faced was extreme, as later fatalities would show.

A Royal Visit

King George VI visited Vernon just twelve days later and awarded the first naval decorations of the war to the men involved. Churchill returned to Vernon in January 1940 to examine the German magnetic mines for himself.

Below: The Shoeburyness mine
Bottom: Mining and MDD men at Shoeburyness

This was a glorious part of the history of the old Gunwharf site. More honours for bravery came at the beginning of the new year and Dr Wood was awarded the OBE in June. The need to master constantly evolving mine technology and to counter mining attacks was to occupy Vernon for the rest of the war and was to be one of its chief responsibilities.

Above: Torpedo test launching
Below: King George VI at Vernon in December, 1939

85

HMS Vernon: a centre for science and technology in times of war

Although each nation had, and retains, military academies (for example, the British Royal Naval Academy (later College), Portsmouth, 1733-1806, the Royal Naval College, Greenwich, 1873-1998, and the present-day Britannia Royal Naval College, Dartmouth), until the 20th century there were no national scientific military establishments. Even in the First World War scientists often enlisted in the armed services; but, following the loss of Henry Moseley and others in battle, efforts began to steer scientists and technologists into warfare research.

Henry Moseley, a brilliant physicist who had worked with Nobel-prize winning Ernest Rutherford at Manchester, had chosen military service and was killed tragically by a wartime sniper's bullet in Turkey in 1915, aged just 27. This was a great loss to Britain and to science, bringing about the change in policy.

Albert Wood, another brilliant physicist from Rutherford's team, chose instead and at Rutherford's suggestion, to join the 1915 Admiralty Board of Invention and Research (BIR); he was one of the first two scientists to do so.

Wood said the formation of BIR was 'a landmark in the history of the Navy'; it was formed to secure 'expert assistance in organising and encouraging scientific effort in relation to the requirements of the Naval Service'. The Admiralty Experimental Station (AES) was set up by the Board in 1915, becoming the Admiralty Research Establishment (ARL) in 1921, enjoying purpose-built premises next to the National Physics Laboratory, Teddington.

These institutions were staffed by a formidable group of scientists. Over the years they included not only Wood and his Rutherford laboratories electrical engineer colleague, Harold Gerrard, but Nevill Mott (winner of the 1907 Nobel Prize for Physics), George Deacon (chemist and oceanographer), Harrie Massey, David Bates, and John Gunn (all mathematicians and physicists), Robert Boyd (founding director of the Mullard Space Science Laboratory), and, most well-known, Francis Crick (1962 Nobel Prize for Physiology or Medicine, and discoverer, with James Watson, of the structure of DNA).

Albert Wood, OBE DSc   **Henry Moseley**

The Admiralty's Mining Design Department at HMS Vernon, with its Mining and Torpedo Schools, had close connections with the AES and ARL. During the Second World War, Wood, Mott, Massey, and Gunn all carried out work at Vernon: experimentation and the trials of countless devices and systems were all undertaken by these civilian scientists, working with specialist naval officers. They formed part of Winston Churchill's 'war lab', born out of his imaginative mind and the advice of Professor Frederick Lindemann. The importance of this work, scientific and technical, can hardly be exaggerated; as a result the 'battle of mines' and many more wartime struggles were won. The HMS Vernon schools undertook expert training in all aspects of mine and torpedo warfare, countermeasures, and naval electrical installations.

Albert Wood (1890-1964) became Chief Scientist at Vernon from 1937 to 1943. His work included mine development, German mine analysis, and countermeasures. He became Deputy Director (Physical Research) at the RN Scientific Section from its inception in 1944. His naval counter-part at Vernon, the gallant Commander John Ouvry, said that Wood 'rendered great service to his country over a long period'.

Scientific research for the Navy, along with the other armed services, continues, making even more use of civilian expertise. One of the establishments is the Defence and Scientific Laboratory on Portsdown Hill, not far from the old Vernon site.

The Blitz

The Royal Air Force had been successful in clearing the day-time skies in the Battle of Britain. The next phase of the war, the night-time Blitz, started in September 1940

Massive strategic German air attacks, known as the Blitz, were concentrated on London and other heavily populated areas as well as factories and docks. There was considerable work for the Vernon teams in Portsmouth deactivating the large number of mines - used as bombs by the Germans - that had failed to explode.

Vernon hit

HMS Vernon and the dockyard had taken their first hits in lesser, earlier air-raids on 24 August 1940 when the Alexandra building (electrical instruction) was damaged. Further raids in December finished off Alexandra and damaged the Warrior building causing two deaths and numerous injuries. One of the biggest raids of the Blitz occurred on 10 January 1941 when thousands of incendiary and hundreds of high-explosive bombs were dropped on Portsmouth. A major casualty was the power station next to Vernon. Many bombs struck Vernon that night and buildings were damaged - some beyond repair. The clock tower on the Vulcan building, the old 1814 Grand Storehouse, was struck and totally destroyed but the Vernon firefighters, using water from the creek, were able to confine the fire to the tower. The Captain and Commander's houses were hit and Vernon was out of action for several days.

The site endured further serious air-raids that year, the worst of which was on 10 March when seven high-explosive bombs landed on Vernon. The Dido building, which at the time was one of the ARP (Air Raid Precautions organisation) headquarters, was very badly hit. One hundred and forty people were buried in the rubble, about a hundred of whom were killed.

Constant interruptions from air-raids hindered the nationally vital mine investigation

work, as well as the equally important mining torpedoes and electrical systems training and trials. It was decided to evacuate the site.

1 **Bomb damage inside Warrior building**
2 **Destruction of Vulcan clock tower, 10 January, 194**
3 **First bomb to hit Vernon (near Alexandra Building), 24 August 1940**
4 **Destruction at Electrical Experimental Department building, 10 January 1941**
5 **Shrapnel damage to Nelson Gate retained after conservation as a historical record**

Left: Firefighting in Portsmouth during the Blitz
Right: A plan showing bomb sites in Gunwharf area

HMS Vernon evacuated

Leigh Park, Hampshire

Many sections moved out of Vernon between September 1940 and March 1941 - the Mining Design Department being one of the first, relocating to the grand Leigh Park House, just north of Havant. Other Departments and sections were assigned to sites in Hampshire, Weymouth, Weston-super-Mare, Carlisle and Scotland. A decision in March 1941 to evacuate Vernon substantially meant that accommodation had to be found for the extensive training and administration departments. Roedean Girls' School, in Sussex, having evacuated its girls and staff to the Lake District, was assigned, under a commanding officer, as Vernon's main headquarters with other sections located nearby.

However, the Portsmouth Gunwharf site, was still used and had its own commanding officer. Work continued in the mining shed and in the Controlled Mining section at the nearby Lennox Garage. The Command Fire Fighting School was maintained on site as well as a mine disposal team, the men living in the accommodation blocks. The Portsmouth Vernon was administered from Roedean and, although things were very different, the same spirit remained.

In 1942 the MDD at Leigh Park designed the MX box for circuits controlling different types of mine detonation such as magnetic, acoustic and combined magnetic/acoustic systems. It enabled detonation methods to be changed in response to constant modification in German mine-sweeping. These were assembled in the machine shop of the large, bomb-damaged MDD workshops at Vernon by a well-trained workforce of about sixty Wrens (Womens' Royal Navy Service), who had returned from Brighton in January 1943. The women also contributed to life at Vernon during its difficult years.

Roedean School, Sussex

Wrens assembling MX boxes at Vernon, Portsmouth

HMS Vernon Department or section	New home
Mining Department (testing for service); Mine Design Department - research and design of material/devices); Mine Design workshop	West Leigh House, Havant (close to MDD) From Commercial Chambers building (c1937) in Portsmouth city centre to Leigh Park House, Havant Hinxman's Garage, Fareham
Electrical Department	East Leigh House (also Havant)
Mining Trials	Arrochar, Loch Long - moored mines; Weston-super-Mare - ground (sea-bed) mines.
Controlled Mining Department	Hillside House, Purbrook (near Havant) and Lennox Garage, Southsea
Whitehead Department	RN Torpedo Factory, Alexandria, Argyllshire
Whitehead Trials staff	Carlisle
Torpedo trials	Loch Long, Argyllshire/Dunbartonshire, and Stokes Bay (near Gosport) and (HMS Osprey) Weymouth (aircraft torpedo trials and ship building)
Mine Sweeping Department; Future sweeps	Kimmerghame House, Fettes College, Edinburgh
De-gaussing section	Old Assembly Rooms, Clarence Pier, Southsea, and then elsewhere
Instructional Book Production Department	Ryecroft, Ropley, (near Arlesford, Hampshire)
Training* and Administration (*especially electrical and Whitehead)	**Roedean Girls' School**, near Brighton Known as Vernon(R) White ensign hoisted 31 May 1941
High power electrical practical workshop; Whitehead instructional workshop	Grand Garage, Brighton Dreadnought Garage, Brighton
Vernon's Womens' Royal Naval Service ('Wrens')	John Howard Home for Old People, Brighton
High power electrical instructional facilities, Sub-lieutenants' quarters, Central pay accounts	St Dunstan's Home for the Blind, Ovingdean (near Brighton)
Chief Petty Officers' and Petty Officers' quarters	Childrens' Summer House, Rottingdean (near Brighton)

New plans for HMS Vernon

'At the 858th meeting of the Finance Committee the view was reaffirmed that the rebuilding of HMS Vernon....should proceed as quickly as possible' Admiralty Civil Engineer-in-Chief Meeting Notes, November 1944

In 1944 it was decided that a radical new plan was required for the whole Vernon establishment. Its work had become highly important but the site and its war-damaged buildings were in a poor condition and more modern facilities were needed for a new era.

New plans

Plans were drawn up for redevelopment of the site with existing buildings repaired and used where possible. Although it had to be built economically, the Admiralty wanted the new buildings to form 'a pleasing and balanced architectural composition' with facades being well-designed 'in keeping with the high purpose of this important naval establishment'.

The whole scheme was to be completed by the end of 1947. Accommodation for 77

Officers, 40 Warrant Officers, 500 Chief Petty Officers/Petty Officers, and 520 ratings wa planned for Old Gunwharf. Offices, lecture rooms, laboratories, workshops, drill shed swimming baths, squash courts, gymnasium garages, church, cinema, captain's residence and a wharf for two destroyers were to be or the southern half. The MDD was to remain at Leigh Park where it became the Admiralty Mining Establishment.

Demolition and historic buildings

Demolition for Stage 1 got underway at the beginning of 1945. By April the MDD workshops, the historic Vulcan north wing and all buildings west of Vulcan had been swept away. Although the Admiralty was interested in

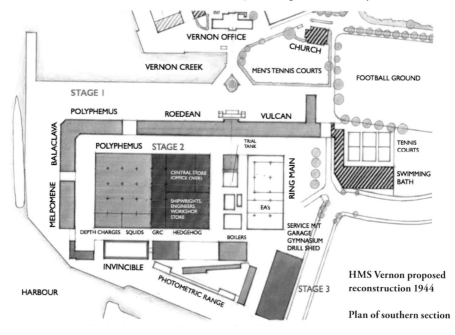

HMS Vernon proposed reconstruction 1944

Plan of southern section

Sketch of Creasy instructional building, 1956, in place of 1944 proposals

the architectural quality of the redevelopment, this did not extend to the retention of significant historic buildings.

The 1944 Town and Country Planning Act, establishing the listing of buildings of architectural or historic interest for the first time, had just become law but the conservation movement had to wait many more years before the Act had 'teeth'. Historic buildings were not on the Vernon agenda.

Despite being part of the demolition programme, the early 19th century Infirmary building and other adjacent structures were left standing. The reason is unknown.

Building work commences then stops

Foundation piles for the Stage 1 buildings were driven into the ground and completed by early 1946. The whole programme then came to a halt on the appointment of Captain John Hughes-Hallett. He was given the even more important and urgent task of forming a combined Torpedo and Anti-Submarine branch (TAS) at Vernon. As a result, the large Creasy building (above) was not started until the mid-1950s.

Had the massive 1944 operational complex and accommodation blocks been built, Vernon would have been, apart from the old administrative offices building, Nelson Gate and some fabric of just two other buildings, a wholly twentieth-century development. A Gunwharf Quays development would have looked very different.

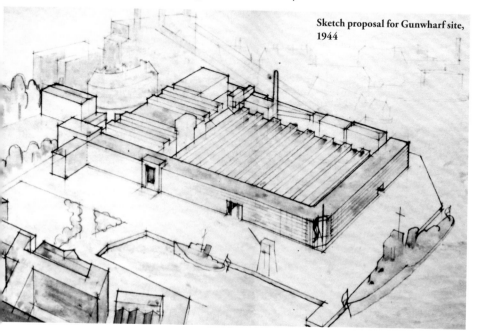

Sketch proposal for Gunwharf site, 1944

Post-war reality

In 1947 a new Torpedo and Anti-Submarine branch (TAS) was formed taking over the whole of HMS Vernon and giving Gunwharf a new lease of life

Units started returning to Vernon in 1943 and by the summer of 1946 the homecoming was complete. By then Vernon was a depressing place with drab buildings, poor roads, and an air of despondency. This was the point at which Captain John Hughes-Hallett took command.

Hughes-Hallett not only combined the Torpedo and Anti-Submarine branches but also set about reordering the site and establishing discipline which had become lax. TAS comprised three new departments: Administration, Instructional, and Sea Trials and Development. The branch was fully functional in 1950 and there was 'a new and brisker tempo of life at Vernon'. The Electrical Department was relocated at HMS Collingwood, Fareham.

The Cold War

The Cold War era, with its proliferation of nuclear weapons, began around 1947. Although some argued conventional warfare, including naval, was obsolete, non-nuclear systems and methods continued to be developed and instructed. As a result TAS continued at Vernon for nearly fifty years as did mine-warfare training and deep (rather than mine-clearance) diving. Its importance as a centre for mine and torpedo training, including new anti-submarine uses of helicopters and mine-hunting, gave Vernon continuing prominence.

New Buildings

New quarters were erected for Chief Petty Officers, and the four-storey Scott building, named after the celebrated Vernon explorer, for ratings and Petty Officers was built in 1968. The extensive Creasy instructional building was constructed in two phases: 1955/6 and the early 1970s.

Despite all this activity, the new post-wa[r] signalled the end for the old gunwharf as a establishment after 275 years of military hi[story]. As a result of Defence Reviews and rationalisa[tion] TAS moved to HMS Dryad at Southwick in and Vernon ceased to be a separate command [in] March 1986.

Captain Robert Falcon Scott, CVO, (Scott of the Antarctic) 1868-1912

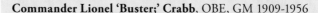

Scott was a naval torpedo officer and explorer who attempted to be the first man to reach the South Pole.

Scott was born in 1868 in Devonport and entered the navy at 13. After 10 years experience at sea a young Lieutenant Scott entered the floating HMS Vernon Torpedo Training School, passing out two years later with distinction and serving as torpedo officer on the depot ship HMS *Vulcan*.

He later met a representative of the Royal Geographical Society which led to an expedition, on the ship *Discovery*, to the Antarctic. A second expedition, with Scott, now Captain, sailing the *Terra Nova*, developed into a race against the Norwegian explorer Roald Amundsen. The story of how he died on the Ross Ice Shelf, aged 43, is well known. His widow, Kathleen, carved a statue of him in 1915. It can be seen in Porter's Garden in Portsmouth's Historic Dockyard.

Commander Lionel 'Buster;' Crabb, OBE, GM 1909-1956

'Whatever may be the circumstances in which he met his death, all of us agree that this country would be the poorer if it were not for men like Commander Crabb.' Hugh Gaitskell, Leader of the Opposition, in 1956.

'Buster' Crabb was an RN Volunteer Reserve diving bomb and mine disposal officer during the second World War who demonstrated legendary bravery deactivating enemy mines in the Mediterranean. During the Cold War, he worked briefly for MI6. He was based at HMS Vernon and met his death in 1956 while carrying out a secret mission. He made a dive into Portsmouth harbour (near to where HMS *Warrior* lies today) where visiting Russian warships, carrying top USSR Communist Party official, Nikolay Bulganin and First Secretary Nikita Kruschev, were moored. The incident caused a major political furore which was highly embarrassing for the British government; questions were asked in Parliament.

Although journalists and friends have tried to investigate this tragedy, a 100-year Official Secrets Act embargo was placed on the most relevant documents. We may never find out how Buster met his death. A mutilated body, not necessarily his, was found over a year later, miles along the coast from Portsmouth.

Top: Creasy building
Above: HMS Vernon, 1997

HARBOUR RENAISSANCE

Southern part of Portsmouth Harbour, 1996

5

Far reaching changes at Vernon

'The period from 1945 to 1979 was one of immense change in British defence policy. By 1979 only a few vestiges of what was once the world's largest empire remained.' Professor Andrew Dorman, King's College, London (2002)

Margaret Thatcher became the British Prime Minister in 1979 at a time of economic decline and industrial unrest. A policy of privatisation for state industries emerged as well as reductions and rationalisation of the civil service, modifications to industrial policy, and trade union reform.

The Way Forward

In 1981 the Secretary of State for Defence, John Nott, published a White Paper entitled *The United Kingdom Defence Programme: The Way Forward*, outlining the Government's intended new defence policy including major reductions in the fleet and the cancellation of ship refits. The news came as a 'bombshell' to the Chiefs of Staff, the military leadership, and had serious consequences for all naval bases. Chatham and Gibraltar were to close altogether (1983 and 1984) and Portsmouth was to be run down substantially: the once proud royal dockyard was down-graded to become the Fleet Repair and Maintenance Base.

The closure of HMS Vernon

The city of Portsmouth could be forgiven for thinking that the 198 Falkland's War in the southern Atlantic, with the navy playing a vital part, might reverse or even just delay some of the intended cutbacks. But this was not to be. The new post war era signalled the end for Gunwharf as a naval establishment. In September 1982 the Government announced that HMS Vernon would close by 1986.

Redevelopment of Gunwharf

In 1975 the Vernon offices, Vulcan storehouse, Royal Marines Infirmary and Nelson Gate received combined statutory protection a Scheduled Ancient Monument No 507. A *Report* by Portsmouth's City Planning Officer in April 1986, explored the benefits of redeveloping the Vernon/Gunwharf site. Ideas included a ferry

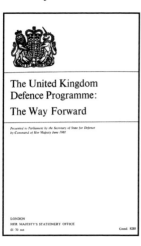

The United Kingdom Defence Programme: The Way Forward

Presented to Parliament by the Secretary of State for Defence by Command of Her Majesty June 1981

LONDON
HER MAJESTY'S STATIONERY OFFICE
£1 70 net   Cmnd. 8288

Scheduled Ancient Monument No. 507
Clockwise from top left:
Vulcan, Infirmary, Vernon Offices, Nelson Gate

Closures resulting from Nott's White Paper:
Left: Priddy's Hard (1990);
Right: Royal Clarence Yard (1991);
Far right: Haslar RN Hospital (2009)

ort, expansion of The Camber fish quay, or a nixed development of residential, office and workshop uses.

HMS Nelson (Gunwharf)

Although the site ceased to be an independent command on 31 March 1986, becoming part of the naval base as HMS Nelson (Vernon site), it still had a role for a few more years. In 1987, it was renamed (again) HMS Nelson (Gunwharf) and briefly became Headquarters for the Commandant General, Royal Marines. The MoD finally announced its plan to release the site, or a large part of it, in 1992/3.

100,000

IS THE NUMBER of people who joined the TUC's March for Jobs in 1981

1981

WAS A YEAR of social unrest with major riots in Brixton (London) and Toxteth (Liverpool)

Employees in Portsmouth Dockyard from World War II

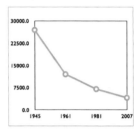

Below: Portsmouth's dockyard workers waiting to hear John Nott break redundancy news in 1982

Visions for the future

In 1990 Portsmouth City Council proposed, in its 10 year Local Plan, a vision for the future including 'exploiting the development potential of the Portsmouth Harbour coastline between Whale Island and Old Portsmouth for docks, transport and tourism uses'. Concern was expressed for the future prosperity of Portsmouth:

'In many ways, Portsmouth is running to a standstill. Further development is required to maintain the momentum that has been built up and to attract the further investment needed to continue the renewal of the City's ageing urban fabric.'

Civic Offices, Portsmouth

Gunwharf was earmarked for uses including offices or light industry, a science park or housing, shops, restaurant, leisure, hotel, and public access to the waterfront.

The Millennium Commission

Three years later Parliament passed the National Lottery etc Act. The Act set up the National Lottery and established the Millennium Commission, with a projected fund of £1.7 billion.

'It [the Commission] will use money raised by the National Lottery to encourage projects throughout the nation which enjoy public support and which will be lasting monuments to the achievements and aspirations of the United Kingdom'

Bids were invited by the commission and as result there were many discussions within local authorities and other institutions throughout the UK about the potential major projects they could put forward which would meet the criteria to attract funding.

Millennium discussions in south-east Hampshire

While on holiday in South Africa, John Vail a senior partner of commercial surveyors Vail

The Still and West, Spice Island

Williams, visited the Victoria & Alfred Waterfront at Cape Town. He thought the development was 'brilliant and exactly what we want in Portsmouth'. He knew the release of the Gunwharf site was imminent and thought the same design principles could be applied.

He and Hedley Greentree, head of architects HGP in Fareham, met for discussions with Paul Spooner, the City Council's Head of Marketing. Paul was especially passionate about bringing more people into Portsmouth and revitalising the city, but the council did not have sufficient funds to purchase the site

Left: Paul Spooner
Right: Hedley Greentree
Far right: John Vail

Could a Millennium grant help to secure the Gunwharf site for Portsmouth?

Late in 1994 the three met in the Still and West pub, Spice Island. Purchasing Gunwharf itself could not come from Millennium Commission funds. Robert Ching the city council's finance director and Ron Wilson of Gosport Borough Council joined the meeting. A major harbour project with Gunwharf as central element was required, funded by a public/private partnership scheme.

To 'win' the funds they needed a big concept - a landmark scheme for the millennium. It had to include other assets such as the historic dockyard and, across the harbour, the Priddy's Hard former armaments depot and Royal Clarence Yard. The scheme must be designed to rejuvenate flagging prosperity caused by the downgrade of Royal Navy operations and include significant benefits for the community and tourism: a vision for the rebirth of Portsmouth Harbour.

The Gunwharf site 'urgently needs a new owner who will restore its historical buildings and put them to a suitable new use'. **Marcus Binney, Save Britain's Heritage, 1993.**

Gunwharf was designated a Conservation Area in 1991. Historic buildings identified by the council for possible retention:

1 Ariadne Wardroom
2 Donegal Lodge
3 Defiance Building
4 Florence Nightingale Sick Bay
5 Shell Magazine
6 Battery Room
7 Office Building

Portsmouth Harbour Millennium Bid

'We are ready to meet the challenges'
Paul Spooner, Portsmouth City Council's Head of Marketing

A grant from the Millennium Commission was vital for providing the infrastructure and public attractions such as a Millennium Walk, museums, road junction changes and a water bus service, which would enhance the waterfronts of Portsmouth and Gosport. The Gunwharf scheme was central to the success of the whole bid, binding it all together and making it a worthy Landmark Project.

Those involved in taking the scheme forward met with Portsmouth City Council's Planning Officer early in January 1995. They understood that because Portsmouth had always been defined by its waterfront it was important, symbolically, to ensure there was significant waterside development for the new millennium, representing a new phase in the city's future.

Millennium Harbour Consortium

The first step was to establish a consortium formed of local stakeholders, including local councils, the Portsmouth Naval Base Property Trust, and the University of Portsmouth. It would bid for one of the landmark projects through the Portsmouth and SE Hampshire Partnership with the city council taking the lead. The design team should be local but an internationally renowned architect should be invited. Consultants would be commissioned and a major construction company appointed.

The final decision to go ahead with a bid was made later that month with the application needing to be submitted by March.

Master Plan

A master plan was essential and would provide a unifying concept for the harbour as a whole.

Working group

The consortium set up a working group with meetings every day at 8.00am in Portsmouth Civic Centre - overnight working was essential. Master plans, briefs, costings, and administrative details were required by the Millennium Commission for what had grown into a £100 million project named the Renaissance of Portsmouth Harbour. Steering and project teams were set up and by February 1995 there were also sub-groups working on the bid in this race against time.

Sketch of LRT train

Towers and tunnels

During January, the idea of a public viewing tower was introduced - a 'landmark' for a landmark project. It proved to be a significant element in the success of the Portsmouth bid.

Another important proposal was a Light Rapid Transit railway system connecting the project with the whole of south east Hampshire. A tunnel for the LRT under the harbour mouth would connect Portsmouth to Gosport and the harbour's waterfronts would be linked by a water-bus service.

The Gunwharf Site

The Ministry of Defence informed the city council that it proposed to place Gunwharf on the market in mid-1995.

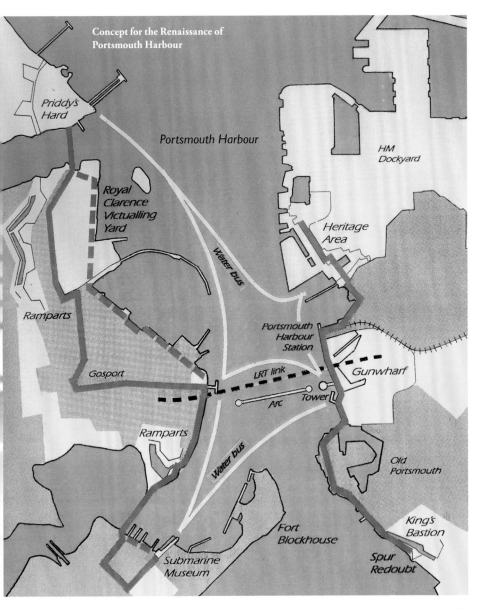

Concept for the Renaissance of
Portsmouth Harbour

Priddy's Hard

Portsmouth Harbour

HM Dockyard

Royal Clarence Victualling Yard

Heritage Area

Ramparts

Water bus

Portsmouth Harbour Station

Gosport

LRT link

Gunwharf

Ramparts

Arc   Tower

Old Portsmouth

Water bus

King's Bastion

Fort Blockhouse

Submarine Museum

Spur Redoubt

Different design approaches

During February and March 1995 a team led by Hedley Greentree produced a series of design options, focussed on Gunwharf. On 16 March there was a presentation to Prince Charles who showed general approval of the concept but was keen to see the Ariadne wardroom building retained. At the same time Sir Michael Hopkins (who had recently won the RIBA Gold Medal for architecture) put his own scheme forward demonstrating a more architectural approach based on a central park.

Left: **Prince Charles at Portsmouth with Hedley Greentree, and consortium chairman, Ben Stoneham, looking on**

Below: **The Michael Hopkins & Partners Millennium project scheme**

1   The Tower
2   Retail Arcade (at The Hard)
3   Ariadne Wardroom block
4   New Park (to city centre)
5   The Arena (Note: scheduled Vernon offices building removed)
6   Creasy Building retained
7   University Campus (based on an incomplete Vulcan building)
8   Extended Ferry Terminal
9   New Bridge
10 The Camber

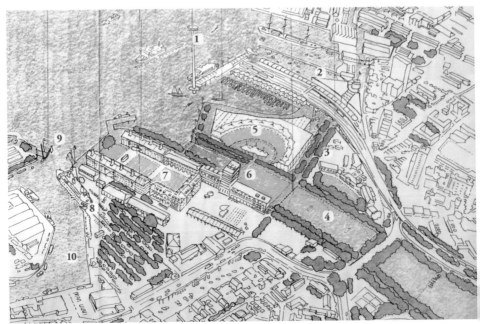

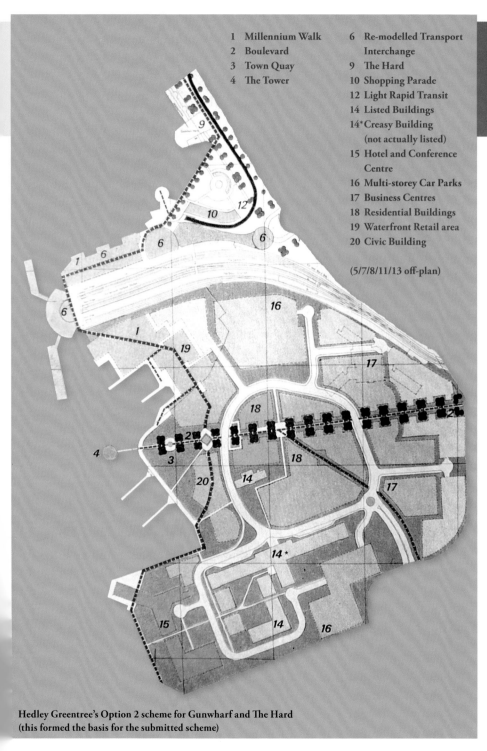

1 Millennium Walk
2 Boulevard
3 Town Quay
4 The Tower
6 Re-modelled Transport
  Interchange
9 The Hard
10 Shopping Parade
12 Light Rapid Transit
14 Listed Buildings
14*Creasy Building
   (not actually listed)
15 Hotel and Conference
   Centre
16 Multi-storey Car Parks
17 Business Centres
18 Residential Buildings
19 Waterfront Retail area
20 Civic Building

(5/7/8/11/13 off-plan)

Hedley Greentree's Option 2 scheme for Gunwharf and The Hard
(this formed the basis for the submitted scheme)

The Renaissance of Portsmouth Harbour Application and Master Plan

'The millennium project will build on Portsmouth's reputation by the provision of new, complementary, attractions and amenities which will win international acclaim and establish Portsmouth Harbour as a world-class tourist destination. The planning, design, development and implementation of the project will also create a national model for urban regeneration.' Application to the Millennium Commission, 28 April 1995

The Masterplan had six themes and six connected elements

Six themes

- recognition of the international maritime role played by Portsmouth Harbour
- creation of a new world-class leisure and maritime heritage destination helping replace dependence on defence work
- uniting the communities of Gosport and Portsmouth by creating a harbour accessible to all and rivalling those of Vancouver, Stockholm and Sydney
- bringing new life to historic buildings and giving public access to the waterfront
- generation of more tourism business for Britain creating 4,000 new jobs locally
- supporting the local community, by a partnership of public and private sectors

Six interconnected elements

- Portsmouth's historic ships and dockyard - enhancing world-class attractions
- two harbour-side promenades
- 100m high harbour tower and a 250m wide illuminated water arc
- the redevelopment and public use of the Gunwharf site, linked to the city centre
- at Gosport, the redevelopment of the historic armaments depot at Priddy's Hard and improvements to the RN Submarine Museum
- waterbus service linking the harbour communities

1	Millennium Tower
2	Water Arc
3	Water Bus
4	The Boulevard
5/8	Renaissance Trail
9	Portsmouth/ Gosport Ferry
12	St George's Barracks
13	Royal Clarence Yard
14	Renaissance Promenade
15	Transport Interchange
16	Car Park
17	RN Submarine Museum
18	Dockyard Heritage area
19	The Hard
20	Transport Interchange
21	New Bus Terminal
22	Gunwharf
23	Listed buildings
25	City Quay

**Master Plan
Revised version
submitted July 1995**

Success for the Renaissance of Portsmouth Harbour bid

Immediately following the Millennium Lottery Fund bid submission there was extensive public consultation on the master plan for the renaissance of Portsmouth Harbour. The consultations included exhibitions in Portsmouth and Gosport, a radio debate and many presentations and public meetings. Portsmouth's daily newspaper, *The News*, also helped generate local enthusiasm.

The chief executive of the Millennium Commission, Jenny Page, was invited to visit Gunwharf and was taken on a special boat trip around the harbour. It was a beautiful day, the royal yacht HMS Britannia was in port and, with the band playing and its sailors looking magnificent, Jenny was captivated by the renaissance vision.

The people of Portsmouth respond

Around 80 percent of the 8,000 visitors to the exhibitions were positive about the project. Although some called for a public inquiry this was not feasible within the programme set by the Millennium Commission.

Success

Success for Portsmouth came on 29 September 1995 when it became one of the first two winning Millennium Fund bids in the country and was rewarded with Landmark status and a grant of £40m*. One of only 14 landmark projects, (others included the Eden Project in Cornwall, Tate Modern in London and Cardiff's Millennium Stadium) Portsmouth received the commission's tenth highest award.

Celebrations

When Portsmouth's marketing manager, Paul Spooner, went to an off-licence to buy champagne to celebrate the bid's success with colleagues, the unwitting shop assistant asked him if he'd won the lottery. And he thought, 'Yes, we have!'

> **Public comments from *The News***
>
> *"I hope it goes ahead. It would be nice to see this area looking good. I think it would be a real attraction. It would be somewhere that everyone would want to visit."*
> Keith Worsfold
>
> *"There is a need to improve the tourist trade. It has been down this year. It would be a unique attraction and very good for the city's image."*
> Debbie Speirs
>
> *"This will take Portsmouth and Gosport into the 21st century."*
> Ann Akers

Millennium Do

* The Renaissance of Portsmouth Harbour grant was £39,142,743 with £823,950 going to Portsmouth Naval Base Property Trust, a total for the Harbour projects of £39,966,693. Nearly £50m had been requested; as a consequence of the reduced amount there had to be some omissions from the proposals and the overall budget was reduced from £113m to £86m.

6,900

S THE NUMBER
f permanent jobs
reated by
Millennium
Commission
unded projects

THE RENAISSANCE OF PORTSMOUTH HARBOUR

The News

WN OF A DREAM

ium project for Renaissance of Portsmouth Harbour   Wednesday, July 12, 1995

Headline from *The News'* special colour supplement

t £604m)   Tate Modern, London (Grant £51.4m)   Eden Project, Cornwall (Grant £59.4m)

Gunwharf for sale

HMS Vernon, the old gunwharf, closed its gates for the last time on 1 April 1996

Although the redevelopment of Gunwharf was not itself included in the Millennium Fund bid and was to be undertaken by a private sector developer, it was, with the tower, a fundamental part of the overall renaissance concept. From the spring of 1995 Portsmouth City Council had been working on its own approach and in November published two briefs:

Gunwharf / Millennium Development Brief envisaged a high-quality mixed-use development creating a 'vibrant festival atmosphere', ready for the millennium, with a good level of retention of historic buildings and reference to archaeology.

Millennium Tower Development Brief set out the tower's importance as a UK landmark for visitors arriving by sea as well as a focal point for the project. A viewing platform at least 125m above quay level was expected, together with visitor areas and decorative and safety illumination.

HMS Vernon on the market

In November 1995, mine-warfare training was transferred to the School of Maritime Operations (SMOPS) at HMS Dryad, Southwick, and the Superintendent of Diving and his sections moved to Horsea Island at the north end of the harbour. Tenders for the purchase of the site were invited in January 1996 by the Defence Estates Organisation on behalf of the MoD.

Portsmouth Harbour Renaissance Limited

The renaissance enterprise was highly complex with many parties involved and the Millennium Commission required a single legal body to receive the grant and to manage the project. An existing Portsmouth City Council company, Eastney Depot Limited, was renamed Portsmouth Harbour Renaissance Limited (PHRL) and began to take overall control for scheme delivery.

A Master Plan for Gunwharf

The July 1995 Master Plan became the key over-arching document for the renaissance project. Now a comprehensive, well-conceived master plan was required for the Gunwharf site. This became the priority of PHRL at the end of 1995 and into 1996.

Gunwharf Quays Summary Document, March 1996

Prospective purchasers and developers were given a copy of a *Summary Document* in March 1996 for the 'development opportunity'. It outlined the requirements that would be placed on developers as well as the criteria to be used in evaluating 'expressions of interest' in order to arrive at a short-list of site purchasers or partners. Details were given regarding the method of sale, land titles, site constraints, and the key importance of the council's November 1995 development briefs.

By order of The Secretary of State for Defence

GUNWHARF *Quay* PORTSMOUTH

FOR SALE

Approx. 12 Hectares (29.64 Acres)
An Unrivalled Opportunity to Create A Festival Waterfront Development

**Suggested design for Millennium
Tower in Development Brief
(HGP) Colour by author**

111

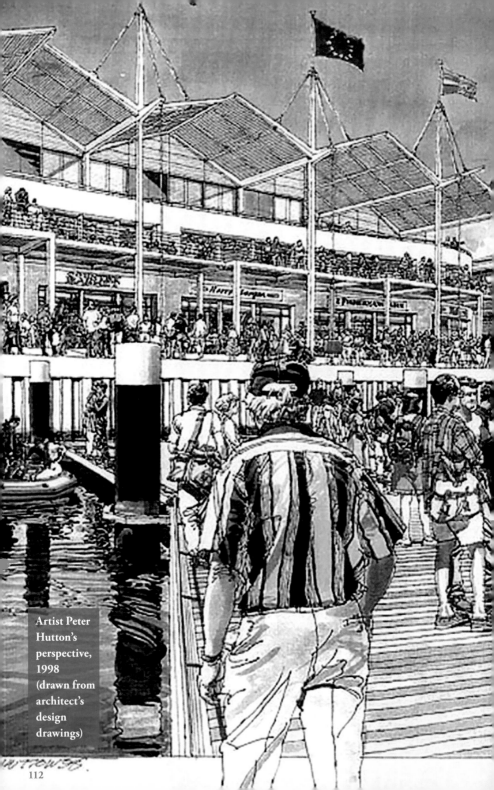

Artist Peter Hutton's perspective, 1998 (drawn from architect's design drawings)

DESIGN & DEVELOPMENT

6

Urban Waterfronts

Waterfront developments as tools for urban reconstruction and regeneration

from Grant and Scott, Urban Forum, 1996

The strong relationship that had existed before the 19th century between dockyards or ports and their towns or cities had been broken in the later stages of the industrial revolution and during industrial expansion. In the 1980s, with many previously bustling urban waterfront sites now derelict, came the realisation of the need to re-establish that relationship.

Developments in retailing in North America during the second half of the 20th century, providing a 'festival marketplace' in a safe downtown environment, were the inspiration for many early waterfront transformations. The concept was rapidly exported around the globe.

Victoria & Alfred Waterfront, Cape Town, South Africa

Plans to restore the connection between Cape Town and its waterfront began in 1984. The proposal was to retain its function as a working harbour but to integrate retail, tourism, and residential land uses. The first development of this type and scale in Africa, it was built in phases from 1989 and finally completed in 2006.

Victoria & Alfred has become one of the continent's most popular visitor destinations. In a beautiful setting beneath Table Mountain, it has a wide variety of shopping (388 retail tenants), markets, restaurants, hotels, museums, and a marina, as well as residential accommodation. A number of historic buildings have been retained. On average since 1997 it has had 20 million repeat visits each year, making it a massive success.

Victoria & Alfred Waterfront, Cape Town, South Africa

Links to Gunwharf

The owners and managers of this development were able to provide consultancy advice* to waterfront developments worldwide - including Gunwharf. They stressed the importance of maximising and enhancing the benefit of the waterside aspect of the location; 'partnership' leases for retail tenants; high standards of safety, parking, customer care and cleanliness; a good range of entertainments and an excellent overall ambience. These became important characteristics of Gunwharf Quays.

Right: Gunwharf Quays from Gosport

Harbor Place, Baltimore, USA

Pier 39, San Francisco, USA

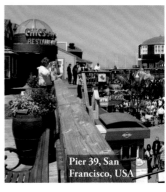

Pier 39, San Francisco, USA

*Including Trevor Blow and Steven Hassel who formed Lordland Property Holdings in South Africa in 1986, becoming core consultants at V&A and, from 1992, managing agents of the retail element. Starting with the belief that the world was their market place, they narrowed their search for a new business venture using the following criteria: it had to be in an English speaking, democratic country with a capitalist economy - and a cricket team! They say they settled on Gunwharf as England had the best cricket team at the time.

A developer for Gunwharf

Final bid document

John Vail, of Vail Williams, who had been inspired by his visit to the Victoria & Alfred Waterfront in South Africa, knew the directors of house developers Berkeley Group and discussed his ideas for Gunwharf with them.

The Berkeley Group

Berkeley's founder and chief executive, Tony Pidgley, future chairman, Roger Lewis, and commercial director Rob Tincknell visited Gunwharf. The old MoD site provided them with an opportunity to put into practice a recent decision to move away from volume house building on 'greenfield' sites and focus instead on redeveloping urban 'brownfield' sites (old industrial land).

They were certainly interested in Gunwharf. The sight of the Ark Royal aircraft carrier sailing past helped Tony Pidgley envisage its potential as a visitor destination and in April 1996 Berkeley put in a bid to buy the site. If their bid was successful they would have to pull out all the stops to deliver such a major scheme as it was one of their earliest mixed-use developments. The Berkeley Group was one of six short-listed for the second round.

Lordland Property Holdings CC

Lordland, the South African managing agent for the Victoria & Alfred Waterfront, was also interested, and one of the directors, Trevor Blow, had visited Gunwharf in 1995. As a consequence Lordland also submitted a first-round bid. If successful it would need a financial partner as an initial idea of forming an association with the Land Securities property group did not materialise.

"[greenfield development] … is building boxes on greenfield sites and the other, [brownfield development] is a far more complicated form of business.

If we are building on the River Thames in London, we are probably dealing with the Port of London Authority, the National Rivers Authority, the Environment Agency. We will probably have marine walks on the frontage of the Thames. We could well be in a Conservation Area and we might well have an archaeological dig. We could be in a listed building and there will probably be basement car parking.

All buildings will be designed by architects and there will be complicated engineering. There will be rights of light problems, red route problems; you name it - this is a study in complicated development.

The project management skills are totally different to those needed for greenfield development."

Roger Lewis speaking in 2001

Above: Tony Pidg[...]

Below: Gunwharf Land Use Sketch from bid documen[...]

Reside[...]

Left: Roger Lewis
Right: Trevor Blow
Far right: Steven Hassel

Berkeley bid, in association with Lordland

For the second-round bid Berkely and Lordland worked together. With its extensive mixed-use waterfront development experience, Lordland was able to made an important contribution.

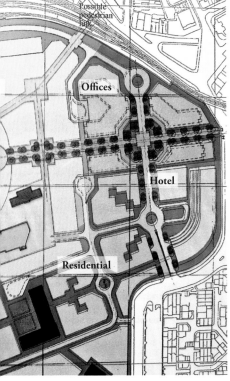

Berkeley Homes was founded in 1976 in Weybridge, Surrey, by Tony Pidgley and Jim Farrer. In its first four years it built four houses and made a 17% profit on a turnover of £121,000. By 1985, as a result of a focused approach to housing development, it had become a fully-listed group valued at more than £67 million. The FTSE 250 Index Berkeley Group Holdings plc has become 'one of the most prominent and successful developers in the UK'. It focuses on London and south east England.

Berkeley's Roger Lewis visited the Victoria & Alfred Waterfront development. The Berkeley/Lordland team submitted a successful bid at Portsmouth City Council offices in June 1996 and a final submission was made in August. The bid document stated:

> 'We believe the Gunwharf offers an outstanding opportunity for the community and all involved in the whole Portsmouth Harbour area to be in the forefront of international attention in the twenty-first century.... We and our team have an unrivalled knowledge of the needs of the city of Portsmouth and of the ingredients to create a commercially viable, lively and popular waterfront mixed development. We are ready to work alongside the MoD and all the parties involved in realising this complex, but unique opportunity'.

It continued:

> 'Lordland has been seeking a site on which another waterfront development, designed and managed to the highest international standard, could be created. The Gunwharf site in Portsmouth combines, in Lordland's view, all the elements required to become a world class waterfront benefiting a major millennium project'.

This final bound document submission incorporated a number of ideas that had been circulating for some time: substantial underground car parking, strong links with the tower and the provision of some all-year-round weather protection. The most striking difference between this and all earlier Gunwharf plans was a much larger element of retail.

The initial planning application

Millennium Tower

In the autumn after submitting the bid, Berkeley/Lordland, led by Roger Lewis, Rob Tincknell and Steven Hassel and their design team, started on a development master plan for Gunwharf. They adopted the 'festival waterfront' urban design concept and many design principles used at Cape Town, broadly following their August land use scheme. Architects from MLH Architects (South Africa), designers of the Victoria & Alfred Waterfront, were an important part of this process alongside HGP. Schemes now being designed started to establish the form and scale of the future development. Some aspects, however, ran counter to the 1995 plans: the Millennium Boulevard, for example, was shortened, and the inclusion of historic buildings and archaeology kept to a minimum.

Heritage Open Days
In September 1996, The Portsmouth Society organised a Heritage Open Days event at the Gunwharf site. Public response to its questionnaires showed unanimous recognition of the importance of Gunwharf to Portsmouth and enthusiasm for safeguarding its historic and maritime heritage. But there was limited support for a tower.

Berkeley/Lordland success
On 24 October 1996 the MoD announced that the Berkeley consortium had been chosen as the Gunwharf developer. Unlike other competitors, Berkeley was willing to build and part-finance the proposed Millennium Tower and this was a factor in its success. The company's financial standing in the development sector and its association with Lordland were other advantages. It took until 1998 to complete all the necessary legal agreements and the formation of Berkeley Festival Waterfront Co Ltd.

Waterbus Service

Retail/leisure buildings (design influenced by Victoria & Alfred Waterfront, Cape Town)

Residential block (preventing views between historic Vulcan building and the harbour)

Left: Rob Tincknell
Right and below: Sketches from the special edition of the council's *Flagship* Publication (*distributed to all homes in Portsmouth*) giving details of the Berkeley Group planning application

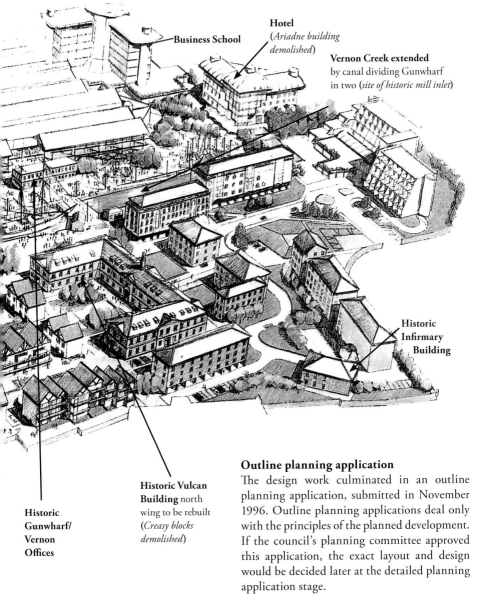

Business School

Hotel
(*Ariadne building demolished*)

Vernon Creek extended
by canal dividing Gunwharf in two (*site of historic mill inlet*)

Historic Infirmary Building

Historic Gunwharf/ Vernon Offices

Historic Vulcan Building north wing to be rebuilt (*Creasy blocks demolished*)

Outline planning application

The design work culminated in an outline planning application, submitted in November 1996. Outline planning applications deal only with the principles of the planned development. If the council's planning committee approved this application, the exact layout and design would be decided later at the detailed planning application stage.

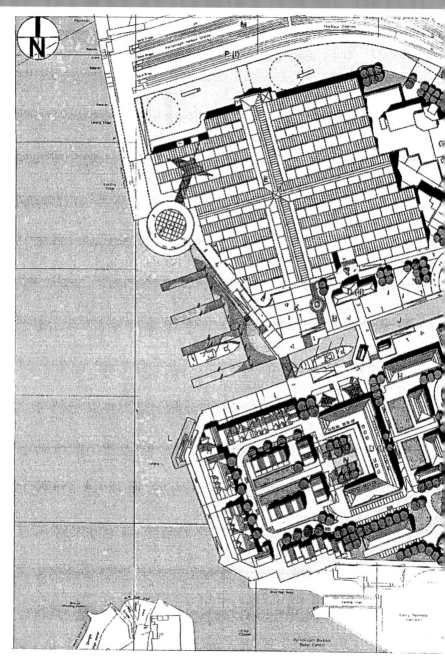

GUNWHARF QUAYS
Berkeley / Lordland Proposal

Key

A   Millennium Tower

B   City Quay

C   Millennium Boulevard

D   Existing Buildings & Features
    D (i)   Vulcan Building
    D (ii) Customs & Excise House
    D (iii) Listed Wall & Gates
    D (iv) Beston's Bastion (partly revealed)

E   Leisure & Retail

F   Hotel

G   Business School

H   Housing

J   New Canal

K   Viewing & Exhibition Area

L   Water Bus Service

M   Transport Terminus, Train, Bus,
    Ferry, LRT

N   Garden Courtyard Areas

P   Site Access
    P (i)   Access from Transport Terminus
    P (ii) Access from Ordnance Row
    P (iii) Pedestrian Access from Gunwharf Road
    P (iv) Service and Visitor Access from
            Gunwharf Road
    P (v)   Residence and Hotel Access from
            Gunwharf Road

The first application master plan,
HGP, November 1996

MASTERPLAN

Scale 0   25   50   100 m   **07**

Responses and revisions

*A consultation process during the early months of 1997
led to new studies, amendments and a
revised application in April*

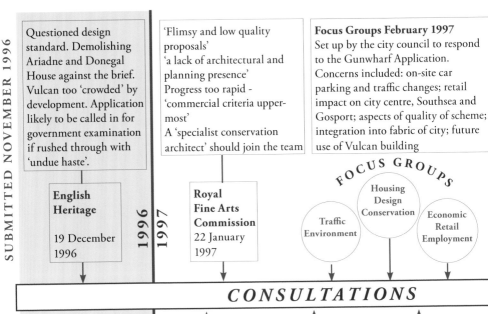

SUBMITTED NOVEMBER 1996

Questioned design standard. Demolishing Ariadne and Donegal House against the brief. Vulcan too 'crowded' by development. Application likely to be called in for government examination if rushed through with 'undue haste'.

'Flimsy and low quality proposals'
'a lack of architectural and planning presence'
Progress too rapid - 'commercial criteria uppermost'
A 'specialist conservation architect' should join the team

Focus Groups February 1997
Set up by the city council to respond to the Gunwharf Application. Concerns included: on-site car parking and traffic changes; retail impact on city centre, Southsea and Gosport; aspects of quality of scheme; integration into fabric of city; future use of Vulcan building

English Heritage

19 December 1996

1996
1997

Royal Fine Arts Commission

22 January 1997

FOCUS GROUPS

Traffic Environment

Housing Design Conservation

Economic Retail Employment

CONSULTATIONS

Lord Palumbo

20 January 1997

Rear Admiral E N Poland

24 January 1997

Portsmouth Society
December/ January 1996/1997

OUTLINE APPLICATION

Lord Palumbo, property developer, former Chair of Arts Council, became Chancellor of Portsmouth University, 1992-2007

Rear Admiral E N Poland author of *The Torpedoman* (about HMS Vernon)

The Portsmouth Society is a voluntary organisation set up in 1973, interested in preserving the best of Portsmouth's environment

The Application contained 'several attractive features', but 'it seems to lack coherence, content, balance and quality'. He wanted the appointment of 'an eminent master-planner' and advocated 'an international architectural competition'.

'I am most anxious that the ancient history of the Gunwharf and of more recent heroic achievements of HMS Vernon should be commemorated in a meaningful way.

Requested public inquiry f Environment Minister. Pleased that: Vernon Creek be extended; good restaura and cafés provided; surface parking limited; north win Vulcan to be re-built. Displeased that: site 'crammed' with new development; not enough waterfront open space; 'a third-rate waste of a world class opportunity'.

Traffic

Design

Commerce

HGP
HGP Greentree
Allchurch Evans Ltd - architects for Gunwharf Master Plan. Recruited architect specialising in conservation from early 1997

GRA
Geoffrey Reid Associates
Appointed by Berkeley early 1997 as architects for retail/leisure sector. Redesigned sector rotating axis through 33°

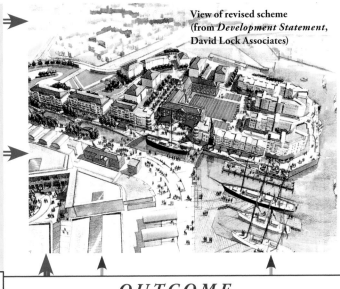

View of revised scheme
(from *Development Statement*,
David Lock Associates)

SUBMITTED APRIL 1997

EXPANDED DESIGN TEAM	*OUTCOME*

HED
Hyland Edgar Driver
Landscape Architects and Urban Designers Appointed by Berkeley in 1996

DLA
David Lock Associates
Town Planners and Urban Designers Appointed by Berkeley in early 1997 to prepare Gunwharf *Development Statement*

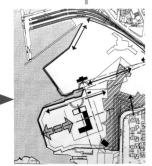

Historic Summary

Concept Layout

REVISED APPLICATION

Designing the retail and leisure sector

Computer image, Central Square

It had been decided from the outset to construct a concrete marine deck between the north quay wall and the railway to increase the retail/leisure area by 40 percent. Constructing a large underground car park was the other factor, releasing yet more space.

A central street

The expanded design team looked at the importance of the pedestrian link from the buses, coaches, trains and ferries at The Hard. It was just one step to the idea of a central street leading down to the waterfront, making finding the way around the site easy and buildings on either side would frame views of the water and passing ships. This brought about a major scheme change: it would have to rotate through 33 degrees.

A unique location

The team wanted to maximise the potential of this unique, historic location within Portsmouth. Its principal aim was to create a new townscape to complement the city.

'In order to achieve this we devised a series of interconnected public/urban spaces. We surrounded these public streets and squares with architectural designs in a variety of styles inspired by the best local architecture.'
(Chris Hacking, Geoffrey Reid Associates)

73
WAS THE NUMBER of unexploded bombs and grenades unearthed during construction

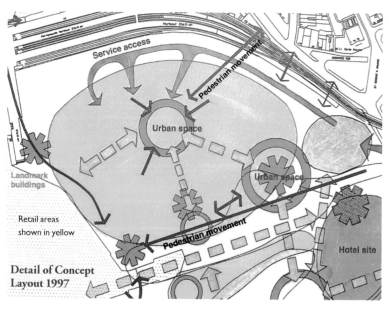

Service access

Pedestrian movement

Urban space

Urban space

Landmark buildings

Retail areas shown in yellow

Pedestrian movement

Hotel site

Detail of Concept Layout 1997

Gunwharf
QUAYS

Chris Hacking

Spice Island and harbour from Gunwharf

Canal

A central square
A 'traditional town square' was located halfway down the street, forming the heart of the scheme and providing a focus of activity for visitors from where everything else radiated. Escalators from the underground car park would bring visitors directly into this central space. The square, landscaped and big enough to have space for events, would be surrounded by fashion shops at ground floor level with wide covered walkways around all four sides providing shelter. Balconies accessing first floor leisure operators also doubled up as viewing platforms.

The **Ground** floor plan

A retail arcade
Coming off the square was a large U-shaped modern interpretation of a traditional shopping arcade with many more shops.

The waterfront
The highlight of the design, the waterfront promenade at the far end of the street, would provide a fabulous setting with bars and restaurants spilling out onto terraces overlooking the harbour, creating a similar bustling atmosphere to other famous waterfronts like Cape Town and Barcelona. The busy traffic of large ships would enhance the experience.

Central street

The Canal
Running parallel to the main street would be the boulevard and the canal, providing additional valuable water frontage and an important buffer zone between the waterside bars and the predominantly residential areas to the south.

Three unique aspects of the new concept
Chris Hacking, believes that there are three unique aspects to this scheme: 1) the historical setting (to bring culture); 2) waterfront maritime activity (to bring life); 3) the blend of uses (to bring commercial success).

The second planning application gets Gunwharf Quays the go-ahead

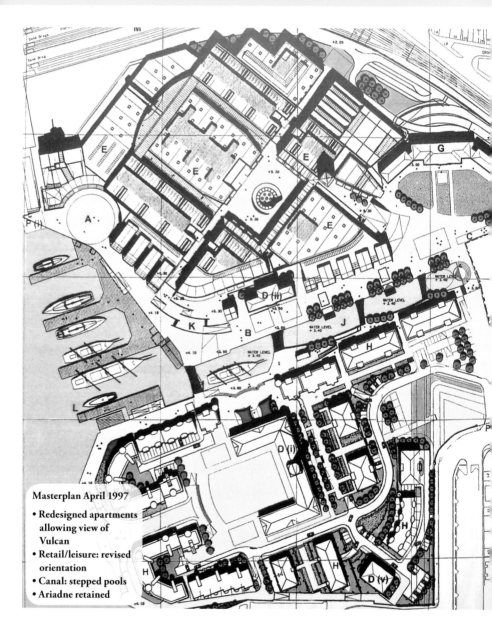

Masterplan April 1997

- Redesigned apartments allowing view of Vulcan
- Retail/leisure: revised orientation
- Canal: stepped pools
- Ariadne retained

1997

WAS THE YEAR
the Labour Party
had a landslide
victory making Tony
Blair Prime Minister

A revised outline planning application, supported by the David Lock Associates development statement, was submitted by HGP on 25 April 1997. Berkeley's original view that this mixed development would prove to be one of the most exciting waterfront schemes, not only in the UK but also internationally, was reinforced.

Development Statement, **April/May 1997**
This study led to a new master plan which was substantially different from the original. Drawings gave details of a new concept for the Vernon Creek canal, comprehensive re-design of the retail area including its re-orientation, retention of the Ariadne building and a better housing layout west of Vulcan. Extensive under-deck car parking, proposals for the Vulcan building, and thoughts on materials and finishes were included. There were also traffic, retail and market appraisal studies.

Market appraisal
Retail
Gunwharf Quays would attract a wide range of socio-economic groups from Portsmouth and the region, counterbalancing the effect of the West Quay shopping development in Southampton. The retail units would be speciality shops, designer outlets, arts and crafts, following the Cape Town model. A total of 90 units and a craft market hall were envisaged.

Residential
The 320 units would range from two-bedroom apartments targeted at first-time buyers to luxury town-houses and larger waterfront apartments. The construction and sale of these houses and apartments would be phased over five years, giving a final completion date of around 2003.

Employment
Research by Portsmouth University indicated that 1,230 full-time equivalent long-term jobs would be created with at least 100 more to maintain the residential and outdoor areas.

Deed of Grant
Meanwhile, the long negotiations between Portsmouth Harbour Renaissance Ltd and the Millennium Commission had come to a successful conclusion and in May 1997 the Deed of Grant was signed starting the release of the grant monies.

Outline planning permission and conditions
The 4th June 1997 was enormously significant in the story of Gunwharf. Two and a half years after the idea of transforming Portsmouth Harbour was conceived, Portsmouth City Council planning committee gave outline permission for the plans for its central component, Gunwharf Quays.

This outline permission, however, was subject to 37 conditions, the most important of which was that the Secretary of State might need (because of the significance of the site) to examine the scheme in detail before giving it his go-ahead. Such a move would automatically trigger a public inquiry, substantially lengthening the whole programme and putting millennium lottery funding at risk.

Should there be a public inquiry?

Criticism of the scheme gave rise to the danger of it being 'called in' for a public inquiry and a long delay

Government coat of arms

The day after the planning resolution (and following his attendance at the opening of the new School of Architecture at Portsmouth university) the architect, Lord Richard Rogers, sent a letter to John Prescott, Deputy Prime Minister, with a copy to Portsmouth City Council saying:

> *'I was shown a development [for Gunwharf] that I believe will destroy the area and more specifically the historic Gunwharf'*

A very concerned Paul Newbold, Portsmouth council's planning officer wrote back immediately, sending a copy to John Prescott and the Government Office of the South East (GOSE), saying:

> *'I very much regret that you have chosen to write without discussing this matter with me....'*

Within a few days, local MP Syd Rapson, the School of Architecture's Sir Colin Stansfield Smith and council leader Leo Madden, had all written in support of the scheme and against a public inquiry. Nick Gurney, the council's chief executive, met with Minister of Planning Nick Raynsford later in the month. Briefing notes prepared for the chief executive on 23 June stated:

> *There is a small but vociferous hard core of objectors based around the Portsmouth Society. They have been lobbying very hard at national level. Neither Lord Palumbo nor Lord Rogers have discussed their opposition to the scheme with the city council. Initial concerns about the quality of the development have been addressed. English Heritage is satisfied with the outline*

proposals and Colin Stansfield Smith has written to acknowledge that progress has been made.

The day after the meeting, GOSE wrote to Paul Newbold:

> *'... the Secretary of State has decided not to intervene and Portsmouth City Council is hereby authorised to decide the application as it thinks fit'.*

There was wide relief at this decision. It meant that now the Gunwharf Quays scheme and the whole harbour renaissance project could proceed without delay.

Correspondence

Archaeology

A full archaeological evaluation* was carried out

Right: Section of Sea Line wall

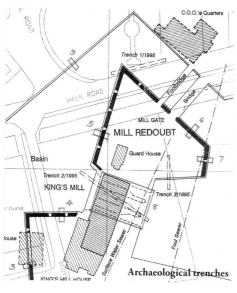

Archaeological trenches

Archaeological trenches

Site excavations took place in August and September 1997 and as a consequence the layout of the development was modified and the foundation design of some buildings changed to avoid damage, particularly to the Mill Redoubt.

Excavation work and research revealed:

1 no remains of Beeston's Bastion survive - the fortifications in this area were levelled in the 1870s;

2 Mill Redoubt exists 600mm or more below ground level; the 'sea line' wall (forming the outside wall of the town moat) also exists - parts are built into the Infirmary Building and exist beneath it; the Vernon Creek Basin was filled in 1920s;

3 the King's Mill was completely demolished in the 1870s - the eastern sluices and western openings survive - the mill pond filling was undertaken between 1876 and 1878;

4 sections of parts of original quay walls of Old Gunwharf and New Gunwharf survive.

It was recommended that the Old Gunwharf and New Gunwharf quay walls should be *'preserved and protected throughout their (existing) length but the preservation of Beeston's Bastion has been found to be unwarranted'*. The idea of representing Beeston's Bastion as a landscape feature was later abandoned. A 'watching brief' (a programme of observation, investigation, and recording by archaeologists, contractors and others on site) was established.

* This was strongly recommended by English Heritage. The Conservation Practice, commissioned by Berkeley, published *An Archaeological Evaluation* in 1997. The project was led by Fred Aldsworth. Gifford supplied archaeological services during the construction period.

Detailed design

The Round Tower

After outline planning permission had been granted* the design team were able to push forward the design process with a view to submitting detailed planning applications before the end of the year. The Berkeley team made an official visit to the Victoria & Alfred Waterfront in Cape Town in August 1997. The South African senior executives provided an insight into the history and development of V&A that the team from Portsmouth found invaluable in their design and planning. Strong links with Cape Town were maintained. Visits were also made to other waterfront developments around the world.

Important Principles
The visit to Cape Town resulted in a list of principles for the retail sector:
- returning the areas of unique waterfront ambience;
- careful tenant selection;
- sustained programme of special events and promotions;
- focus on attracting local residents as patrons and visitors;
- adequate public parking;
- excellent security and public safety;
- high standards of cleanliness and maintenance.

Urban Design
The guiding urban design principles were:
- mixed uses;
- interconnected streets and spaces;
- pedestrian amenity;
- quality;
- scale;
- regard to heritage.

*1997 draft formally granted January 1998

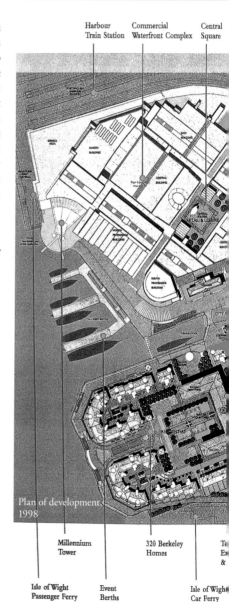

Harbour Train Station · Commercial Waterfront Complex · Central Square

Plan of development 1998

Millennium Tower · Isle of Wight Passenger Ferry · Event Berths · 320 Berkeley Homes · Isle of Wight Car Ferry

Railway arch, outside Gunwharf

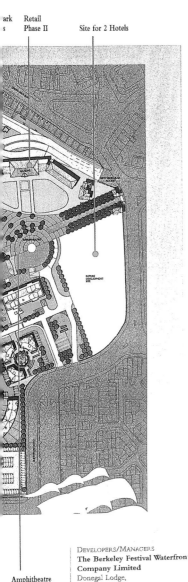

ark   Retail
s   Phase II   Site for 2 Hotels

Amphitheatre

DEVELOPERS/MANAGERS
**The Berkeley Festival Waterfron
Company Limited**
Donegal Lodge,
Gunwharf Quays.

Architectual references

Working on the commercial and leisure areas, Geoffrey Reid Associates looked at the dockyard heritage area, the stone fortifications such as the Round Tower, and Bath Square. The arches to shop fronts were intended to 'reinterpret the arched openings in the naval dockyard and along the perimeter of the site'. The roof within the shopping arcade makes reference to Queen Victoria's railway shelter in the dockyard.

HGP, and PLC Architects (who designed the majority of the final schemes), sought to respond to local Georgian and Victorian architecture in their design of the residential elements, 'avoiding a pastiche of the historic styles' but providing 'a contemporary aesthetic' influenced by them.

Planning permissions

The detailed planning (reserved matters) applications were submitted, and in May 1998 nine applications were approved. These included the retail/leisure sector with its underground car parking; residential accommodation on the south side of the canal; the construction of quays, promenades and boulevards; and a re-built north wing to the Vulcan building together with the reconstruction of its clock tower.

Town House, Old Portsmouth

Town House, Gunwharf Quays

Perspective Views
1 Central Square
3 Central Square
5 Looking west
  from amphitheatre
6 Looking south to
  Vulcan building

Drawings
2 Elevation detail
4 Long elevation of
  main retail street
7 Sketches of town
  houses

1

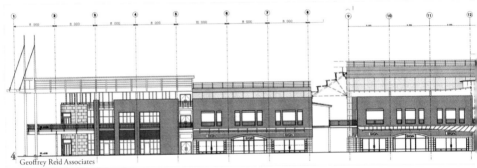

4

Geoffrey Reid Associates

5

6

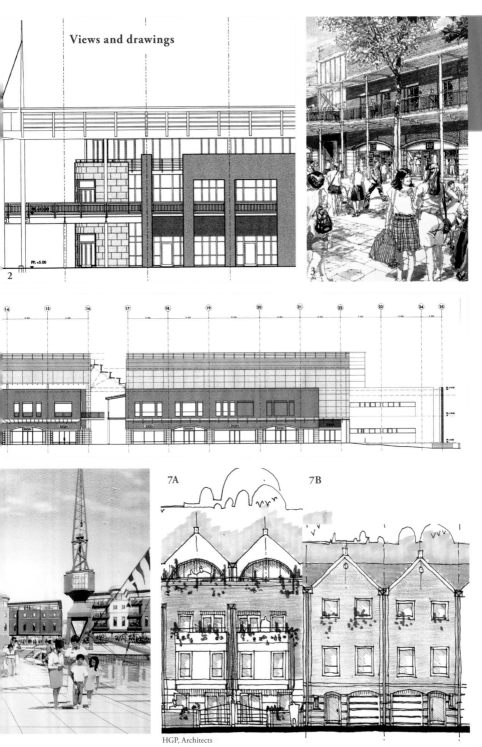

Views and drawings

2

3

7A   7B

HGP, Architects

An architectural competition

Waterfront apartments

Design of the residential blocks west of the Vulcan building received some criticism. In March 1998 English Heritage stated that it was 'wrong for them to dominate and conceal the finest building on the site'. As a result the planning permission process for this area (Waterfront apartments) had been postponed. Discussions involving Portsmouth City Council, English Heritage, the Georgian Group and HGP took place and in the summer of 1998 Berkeley decided to hold an architectural competition for a new approach.

Two local and three national architectural practices were invited to submit proposals (right and overleaf). John Thompson & Partners was successful and planning permission for their scheme was granted in May 1999 (126 apartments, a restaurant and parking for 254 cars).

3, 5
Proctor and Matthews Architects. A London-based practice, founded by Stephen Proctor and Andrew Matthews.

3

6
CZWG Architects. An internationally recognised practice based in London.

4

4, 7
HGP Architects. A Hampshire based practice with offices in Fareham and Leeds. Masterplanners and architects at Gunwharf Quays.

2

1, 2
Architecture PLB. A leading Hampshire architectural practice with offices in Winchester and London.

5

6

7

1

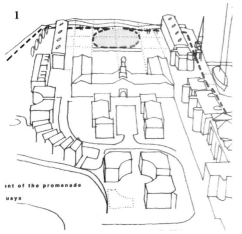

nt of the promenade
uays

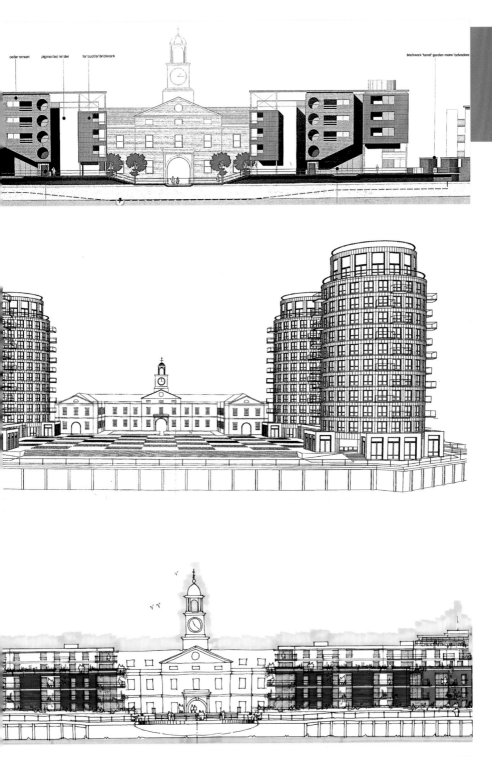

cedar screen   pigmented render   terracotta/ brickwork   brickwork 'turret' garden room/ belvedere

The winning scheme

Waterfront apartments

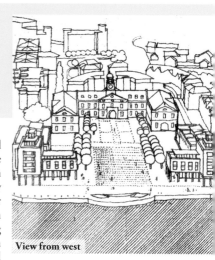

View from west

John Thompson & Partners, a London architectural practice specialising in 'place-making' architecture and urban design, won over the judges with their black and white plans, elevations and lively perspective sketches. Perhaps more than any other scheme, it was designed to allow views through and under the buildings as well as an open setting for Vulcan. The detailed design, and construction drawings of the Waterfront apartments, and housing to the east and south of Vulcan, was undertaken by PLC Architects, Portsmouth, in association with Berkeley design managers.

Elevation showing space given to Vulcan

Waterfront apartments (as built) and Vulcan from the harbour

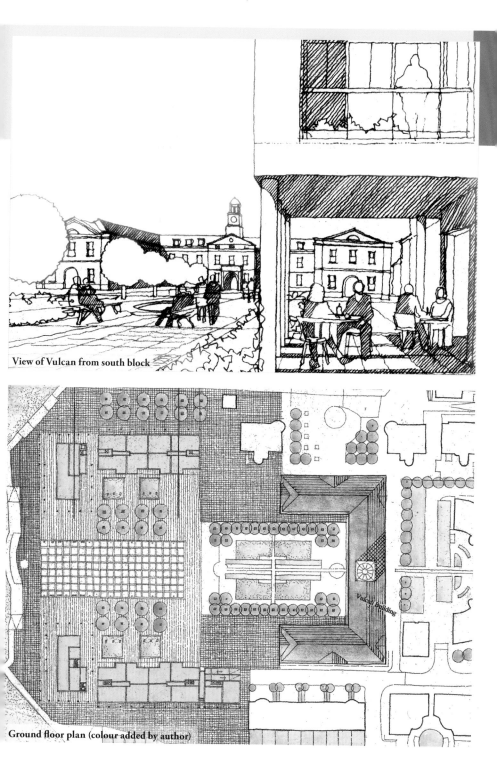

View of Vulcan from south block

Vulcan Building

Ground floor plan (colour added by author)

137

DEMOLITION

EXCAVATION

CONSTRUCTION

CONSERVATION

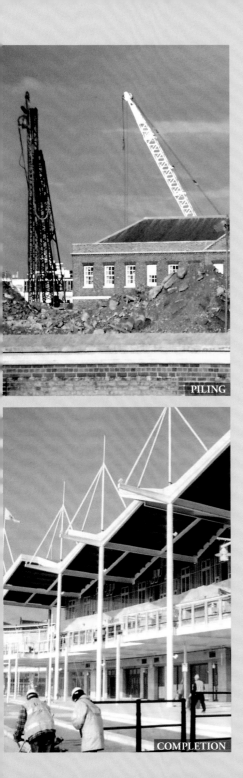

PILING

COMPLETION

CONSTRUCTION 7

Constructing Gunwharf Quays

A fast track programme

In the original 1996 Berkeley bid the overall 'design to completion' programme was compressed into less than four years - an ambitious target. Within this, only 30 months was allocated for the construction of the retail and leisure elements and the early phases of the residential parts. Gunwharf Quays was scheduled to open in November 1999 in time for the year 2000 celebrations.

It was not until autumn 1996 that Berkeley's Gunwharf development team received the go-ahead as 'preferred' developer. Work started immediately, at considerable risk (before purchase of the site and before planning approvals), to prepare studies and submit all the statutory documents associated with such an important redevelopment.

The first stage, involving complex design, planning and legal issues together with sorting out the construction logistics, took two years instead of the planned 12 months. But, remarkably, the construction of the retail/leisure side, including the major civil engineering works of the underground car parks, marine deck and railway arches, took only 30 months as planned. Shops, restaurants and the cinema opened their doors in February 2001.

To complete a scheme of such scale and complexity, so close to its schedule, was a great achievement and is a remarkable story of leadership, management, planning, team work and energy. For many of the principal players involved it was the pinnacle of their careers.

Target dates were amended in 1997 to take account of the two-year design and planning

period: the retail and leisure elements were now to be completed by November of 2000, and the residential and other phases by early 2002, a year later than the original plan.

A fast-track programme for such a complex scheme within the allotted time-span and to

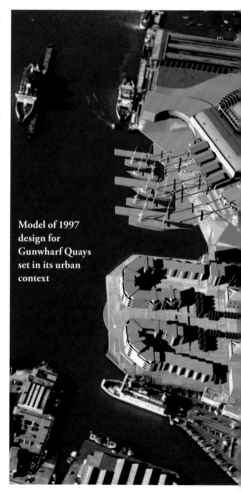

Model of 1997 design for Gunwharf Quays set in its urban context

Richard Thomas

the required quality could not be achieved by traditional procurement methods. A route was selected which enabled key parts of the scheme to be under construction while other elements had not yet been designed. The one downside of this approach was not being able to quantify

precisely from the outset what the project was likely to cost. Costs had to be juggled as the design progressed and further contracts were placed with Berkeley's subcontractors.

For the commercial elements, the design had to be flexible enough to accommodate the demands of the retail, leisure and office tenants whose needs would constantly change to reflect market conditions. Attempting to predict future tenants' needs so early on in the project was a significant challenge. Despite continued efforts by the commercial team, at the start of construction, only a percentage of the commercial tenants had signed up. Therefore key decisions had to be made about how the structure could be designed with sufficient flexibility to accommodate different types and sizes of commercial space.

The most important decision was the layout of the underground car park (750 car spaces on each of two levels), which in addition to its own weight was to take the weight of three levels of commercial development above. A structural grid was adopted, achieving the desired car park layouts, yet providing sufficient flexibility for the retail elements above.

Making these early decisions enabled Berkeley to retain design, time and cost control while maintaining flexibility. Building could begin as soon as each construction package was designed.

Project construction director Richard Thomas, was a key appointment for the project, overseeing the vital 1998 year of preparation and making a positive start with construction in 1999.

A year of preparation

Berkeley commenced demolition knowing that if a Transport and Works Act Order was not obtained radical changes would be necessary to the whole scheme

By the summer of 1998:

Outline Planning Permission had been issued;
Historic building conservation and other reports had been completed;
Detailed Planning Permissions were in place;
Management planning had been undertaken.

But a vital Transport and Works Order, which would give Berkeley the necessary authority to build the development out into the harbour, had not yet been granted. In the face of this predicament Berkeley took the decision to commence site works, with all its associated costs, without the order. Demolition commenced on 10 August, with site remediation following closely thereafter.

Meanwhile the construction management and commercial letting teams had grown into an organisation of 100 by the winter and continued to plan for construction and to procure tenants. This period included the architectural competition and planning application for the Waterfront apartments. Legal agreements were formulated to protect the interests of the two major adjoining neighbours, Railtrack and Wightlink. Railtrack's fragile structures were potentially at risk from subsidence from the large piles which would be installed as close as three metres from their property to create the marine deck.

By the end of the year, architects Geoffrey Reid Associates and civil engineers Mouchel had completed sufficient detailed arrangement drawings of the complex substructure of the retail/leisure scheme for the works to commence. Similar preparations were in hand for the residential southern half of the site.

120,000

CUBIC METRES
of spoil was removed and
transported to Goodwood
to form embankments for
the motor racing circuit

200

WAS THE NUMBER
of lorries on average
needed each day for
16 weeks to remove
all the spoil

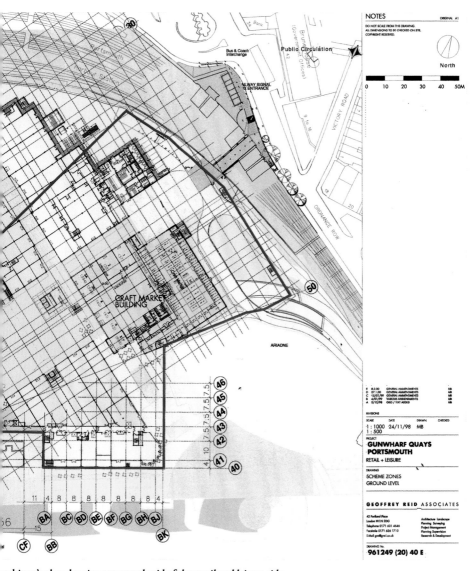

Architect's plan showing structural grid of the retail and leisure side
and the red line of the interlocking piled wall to the basement car park

Demolition

Demolition work started in August 1998 and was completed before the end of the year. The largest building on the site, Creasy, was demolished by two huge hydraulic 'nibblers' in October - it took just four days to bring down the main structure.

1 Ariadne*
2 Donegal*
3 Vernon Offices (Old Customs House pub)
4 Creasy
5 Vulcan (Residential + Aspex Gallery)
6 Shell store
7 Nelson Gate
8 Infirmary building (Residential)
9 Wightlink Ferry Terminal

*later demolished

Foundations for Gunwharf Quays

This unpromising site not only had deep layers of 18th and 19th century infill on mud and gravel beds, but also contamination from its military uses requiring remediation

Large structures often require piled foundations rather than brick or concrete footings. In the Georgian period timber piles were used, while concrete piles were used for the post-war Creasy building. In 1999 the materials were steel as well as concrete.

The southern, residential, half of Gunwharf was the most straight-forward; most of the buildings were built off continuous-flight auger pile deep foundations (bored holes filled with concrete as the auger drill is withdrawn).

More difficult was the northern half where a deep, two-level basement car park structure, the lower floor being well below sea level, was to occupy most of the existing site. The works had to be protected from the ingress of the sea, so an enclosing water-proof 'secant' wall, of more than 2,000 interlocking piles, was installed and the sea wall raised before excavation of the contained ground. A further 1,345 auger piles were bored into the excavated surface providing support for the car park structure and the commercial development above.

Soil investigation at the end of 1997 led to a conclusion that driven steel piling was required for developing the area of harbour between Gunwharf and the railway station pier. As much of the area was in the form of seawater covered mudflats, driven tubular steel piles were the only viable solution. Nearly 370 of these tubes (ranging

from 610 to 830mm in diameter and up to 40 metres long) were driven into the mud, filled with concrete, and capped ready to receive a concrete deck (reinforced concrete beams and planks bound together with a final topping). Piling work on the marine deck started in February 1999 after The Portsmouth Harbour (Gunwharf Quays) Order had been approved by Parliament.

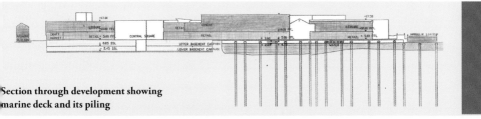

Section through development showing
marine deck and its piling

Progress at summer 1999

Once demolition works had been completed and some of the initial enabling works were underway, construction started in earnest at the beginning of 1999 on both sides of the site. This photograph, taken in July 1999, shows that by the summer most of the underground car park area had been excavated and piled and the car park structure itself was well advanced. The adjacent section of the marine deck - the largest of its kind in Europe - was in progress. It was important that the ground floor deck over the car park and the marine deck were finished concurrently to provide a composite platform for erecting the retail and leisure complex above.

Donegal Lodge
Berkeley Festival Waterfront Co Ltd offices

Construction village
established

Below ground car park decks
under construction following site excavation and piling

'Traveller' piling rigs
working on the marine deck hammering piles into the mud then moving forward on temp beams to drive in the next set

Residential blocks
under construction

Endeavour House
nearing completion
(Marketing Suite)

Tubular steel piles
awaiting barge transport
to marine deck site

Barge with crane
for transporting steel
piles stored on New
Gunwharf to the
marine deck area

Secant interlocking piled wall
on Old Gunwharf enclosing
underground car park area

Progress at spring 2000

Waterfront apartments
excavations and piling underway just prior to final planning approval

Vulcan building
repair of centre block underway

The superstructure for the retail and leisure areas was well advanced but much remained to be done to meet the revised February 2001 completion target.

The future location of the piled foundation structure for the Spinnaker Tower can be seen just to the left of the completed marine deck.

The photograph below shows arcade construction in progress at January 2000.

Former Infirmary building
- conservation and conversion to six apartments completed

Residential blocks
south of Vulcan nearin completion

Marine deck
complete

Steel framework
to retail/leisure blocks
north of Main Street
well under-way

Extended Vernon Creek
ponds under construction

Underground car park
- final section under
construction

Ariadne building
not yet demolished

Progress at summer 2000

The Hard
public transport interchange
for trains, buses, coaches and
passenger ferry

Construction on both Old and New Gunwharves continued rapidly. Meanwhile endeavours were underway to find a new use, such as museum, art gallery or offices, for the Vulcan building.

English Heritage and others advocated retention of the Ariadne Wardroom, an historically important HMS Vernon building. In the end Conservation Area Consent was given for its demolition on the basis of poor structural condition. Prior to demolition, measured building plans were drawn as an historic record. Similar recording was carried out on the old Mill Redoubt and the historic sea walls, all of which were partly exposed during construction and then covered up and retained in situ where practical to do so.

Shopping Mall construction progress (below), June 2000.

Retail and leisure buildings
on marine deck

Railway arch link
to The Hard
structural work
underway

Central Square and
surrounding buildings
under construction

Ariadne
demolished

Donegal
Lodge

Residential blocks
east of Vulcan -
some completed

Waterfront
restaurants
structure in
place

South building
under
construction

Waterfront apartments
ground floor slabs and
underground car park
structure under construction

Vulcan building
under repair;
temporary roof over
south wing

153

All trains stop for Gunwharf

Railtrack agreed to close Portsmouth Harbour station for 52 hours allowing an arch structure to be extended under the track to provide a main pedestrian entrance and link with The Hard

The link between The Hard Interchange and Gunwharf Quays had been an important requirement of Portsmouth City Council from the outset. The construction of this link made use of one of the railway viaduct arches (No. 22) but required a new subway structure on its western side.

Along with the other major construction work which was happening at that time, construction director Richard Thomas and his team had to manage the highly complex task of suspending some of the rail tracks and excavating rubble behind the parapet wall in order to slide in new reinforced concrete subway sections and re-establish the lines.

Preparation for this important part of the railway network required significant planning and an ongoing dialogue with Railtrack engineering teams for over six months before any works commenced. This task had to be carried out within a 52 hour (weekend possession period. Railtrack insisted that if at the halfway stage the work was less than 50 percent complete, construction must stop and everything must be returned and restored back to its original state.

Disruption to the rail network would be significant if the works over ran and hence huge financial penalties hung over Berkeley. The pressure to complete on time was enormous. But in the end the project was achieved with three hours to spare. With the stakes so high and no room for error, for Thomas this meant only three hours sleep during that key 52 hour period.

Pedestrian entrance from The Hard

Suspended rail track with subway units being installed

Subway units with railway arch beyond

Progress at winter 2000

As the original November 2000 target date passed, pressure increased to complete the retail/leisure side by early 2001

In December 2000 the Berkeley Group sold a 50 percent stake in the commercial elements of Gunwharf Quays to Land Securities Group. It sold the remaining 50 percent two years later. The construction team was therefore involved in a major due diligence exercise to satisfy the new stakeholder, while still working intensively to achieve the early 2001 opening date.

The project team liaised closely with the city council's engineers to sort out the logisitics of the delivery of the council's Spinnaker Tower project now that there was only limited access to the tower construction site and that tower construction would not commence until after Gunwharf had opened for trading.

Top left: **Vulcan - temporary roof being assembled**
Left: **Waterfront apartments under construction**

Spinnaker Tower sit
Drilling rig carrying
site survey ready for 2
start of construction

Retail/leisure central area nearing completion

Retail/leisure southern area still under construction

Stothart & Pitt crane on site after refurbishment and relocated

Builders' access road to Vulcan building and Waterfront apartments sites

Hard landscaping underway

Waterfront apartments with reinforced concrete frame and floors nearing completion

Waterfront quay wall under repair

Vulcan building temporary roof over centre block

Gunwharf Quays open

As Gunwharf Quays opened its gates on 28 February 2001, more than 200 queued to be the first members of the public to see behind the Gunwharf perimeter wall for 300 years

Gunwharf Quays opened at 10.10 am on a cold, wet February morning. A jazz band kept the waiting queue entertained as they sheltered in the new subway. First in line Susan Brown, said, "I

just wanted to see what it was like. We've been here about half an hour and we're really excited". Another said, "I think it's going to be brilliant. We've been waiting for something like this for the city for a long time."

More than 1,300 operatives, managers and directors worked through the night painting, clearing the site and preparing shops for opening. By 9.00am the number was 2,000. For many, it was the culmination of the most satisfying project of their careers.

The construction of Gunwharf Quays, at a cost of more than £200m, may prove to be the most significant development of the 21st century in Portsmouth. It changed the direction of the city, raising its profile and giving a massive boost to the economy and its citizens.

Waterside restaurants shortly before completion

The only land-based access to Spinnaker Tower construction site - the 6m width hampered operations for 2001 start of construction

Site for Spinnaker Tower

Roofs to shopping malls completed

Vernon Avenue

Central Square

Ramp to underground car park

Canal completed with bridges (1996 Vernon Creek inlet extended)

Gunwharf Marina

Construction barge

Gunwharf Quays opened and trading

Waterfront apartments still under construction

Conservation

'We plead [with building owners] to stave off decay by daily care, to prop a perilous wall or mend a leaky roof... and to resist all tampering with the fabric or ornament of the building as it stands.'
SPAB *Manifesto*, William Morris, 1877

Conservation

The conservation of a valued historic building or structure, of a 'heritage asset', means all the ways of caring for it so that it retains its historical, architectural and other values (cultural significance). It can include maintenance, preservation, restoration, reconstruction, and adaptation. The idea of caring for historic buildings owes much to William Morris (1834-96), who founded The Society for the Protection of Ancient Buildings in 1877.

When Gunwharf was sold it had many heritage assets - from underground archaeology to listed, or locally important, buildings and structures, and scheduled monuments.

In the 1996 to 2001 construction period of Gunwharf Quays, the skilled care of historic buildings had to be in accordance Planning Policy Guidance PPG15, *Planning and the Historic Environment.*

Conservation Areas

The Gunwharf site formed Conservation Area No. 25. A conservation area is an area of special architectural or historic interest; its character or appearance should be kept or improved. Consent has to be obtained to demolish any building or structure. The Gunwharf Quays conservation area is unusual in that it has more modern, rather than historic, buildings.

The developer, Berkeley, needed to know which buildings had to be retained and which could be demolished in order to plan the site. As there was considerable debate on the matter, a 1997 Conservation Area Consent allowing demolition also retained, strategically, a number of buildings, allowing some work to be planned.

Stothert and Pitt crane

These were: the 1920 Defiance, Nightingale and Actaeon, as well as all the listed and scheduled buildings and structures, the Ariadne wardroom Donegal Lodge, a shell magazine, and a small office building. Consent to demolish the three 1920s buildings, vital for completing the retail and leisure sector, was gained the following year. Finally, and notwithstanding extensive lobbying, the Ariadne wardroom building (also 1920s) received demolition consent in 2000 followed by Donegal Lodge in 2004.

Portsmouth's conservation officer John Pike visited the site in June 1997 and agreed with HGP that certain historic artefacts, including 31 cannons, 5 bollards, two areas of historic paving, and the Stothert and Pitt crane, should be retained.

Old Infirmary House

Gunwharf quay wall, c1803

Left: Old Customs House interior, before repair
Below: Old Customs House interior, after repair
Right: Conservation of Nelson Gate

Left: South wing, Vulcan, before repair
Right: South wing, Vulcan, after repair: Aspex contemporary art gallery (architects, Glen Howells)
Below: Boundary wall, 1803, after repair

Repairing the historic buildings

Defective masonry

For work to start it was essential that the condition of every historic building and structure was carefully examined, making possible the 'detailed programme for each building/structure, including details of their repair and alteration' required by the outline planning permission. Everything had to be approved by the city council and then fully carried out. Berkeley and HGP appointed top conservationists to carry out condition surveys and recommend repairs.

New timber beam sections awaiting installation

Masonry under repair

Masonry

The salty marine environment had weathered much of the stonework and brickwork. Many areas suffered too from impervious cement-based mortar repointing, leading to rain-soaked stones and bricks and frost damage. There was also the unusual damage caused by wartime shrapnel.

Traditional lime mortar, without cement, was used in repairs, allowing the fabric to breath and to accommodate building movement - functions prevented by cement mortar. Shrapnel damage was repaired to shed rainwater and left as part of the building's story.

Timber

Timber decay, caused by insect and fungus attack - both only surviving in timber with a high moisture content - had to be addressed. Oak rot, wet rot, dry rot, white rot, and brown rot fungal attack were found, as was the activity of furniture and deathwatch beetles.

Recommendations included ensuring sound rainwater gutters and pipes, and drainage around the foot of walls. In-depth or surface preservative treatment was applied only to the areas of decay, ensuring effective treatment. This targeted approach is much more successfully than random superficial spraying. Badly defective timber was replaced.

For both timber and masonry attack the most important action was to remove dampness.

Above: Protimeter for basic measurement of dampness
Below: Shrapnel repair, Nelson Gate

Decayed timber tie-beam, Vulcan

Lime-mortar repointing, Vulcan

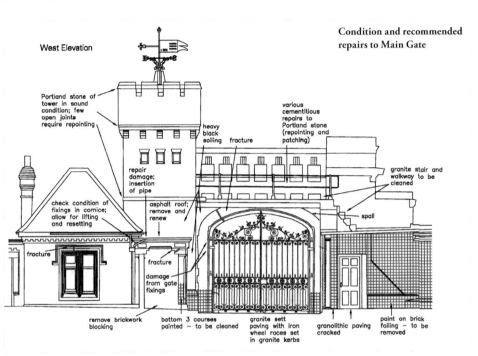

West Elevation

Condition and recommended repairs to Main Gate

Portland stone of tower in sound condition; few open joints require repointing

heavy black soiling   fracture

various cementitious repairs to Portland stone (repointing and patching)

repair damage; insertion of pipe

granite stair and walkway to be cleaned

check condition of fixings in cornice; allow for lifting and resetting

asphalt roof; remove and renew

spall

fracture

fracture

damage from gate fixings

remove brickwork blocking

bottom 3 courses painted – to be cleaned

granite sett paving with iron wheel races set in granite kerbs

granolithic paving cracked

paint on brick failing – to be removed

Main Gate prior to repair

Main Gate after repair

Conservation of Vulcan

By 1996 Vulcan, without its north wing, clock tower and central pediments, was in very poor condition and in danger of significant collapse

Steelwork repairs

The Grand Storehouse, known since 1923 as 'Vulcan', has a central range with two wings, and a clock tower. Enemy bombing destroyed the tower in 1941, and the Ministry of Defence demolished the north wing in 1947. The central Portland stone pediments were dismantled in the 1970s; some sections were stored in the building and reused during conservation.

A two-year programme of repair and reconstruction was carried out for Berkeley under the direction of the author, an architect with HGP, from November 1999.

Main structure

The roof trusses and first floor beams were in a particularly serious condition. Rotten timber had to be replaced with Douglas fir (the original Baltic pine was not available in the sizes required), and steel plates, painted white to match the lime washed building surfaces, brought the structure to a safe standard. Hidden 'flitch' plate repairs (in slots in the centre of beams) were intended but the presence of large wrought iron nails prevented safe sawing of the slots.

At roof level, modern asbestos slates were replaced with natural Welsh slate, and extensive repairs were carried out to dormer windows. Almost all the sash windows were so badly decayed they were beyond repair and had to be replaced with matching units.

Central passageway walls, built on shallower foundations than the main external walls, required underpinning and stitching of the settled brickwork. Brickwork repairs were carried out using specially manufactured imperial-size hand-made bricks. Traditional 1:3 lime mortar was used for brickwork and stone repairs.

Vulcan under repair, 1999

Clock tower

The only records of the clock tower's pre-war appearance were small photographs and an 1855 *Illustrated London News* drawing.

The structure is based on a steel frame, for minimum weight and maximum strength, sitting on the central passageway walls. The timber dome is clad in traditional sand-cast leadwork and the supporting structure is in hardwood and plywood joinery formed around the steel frame. The 3.5 m (11ft 8in) clock faces are mounted on enamelled autoclaved fibre-cement sheets used to reduce maintenance and to mimic the painted metal sheets of the original tower. The clock hands are powered by two tiny synchronous electric motors mounted in the centre of the clock room.

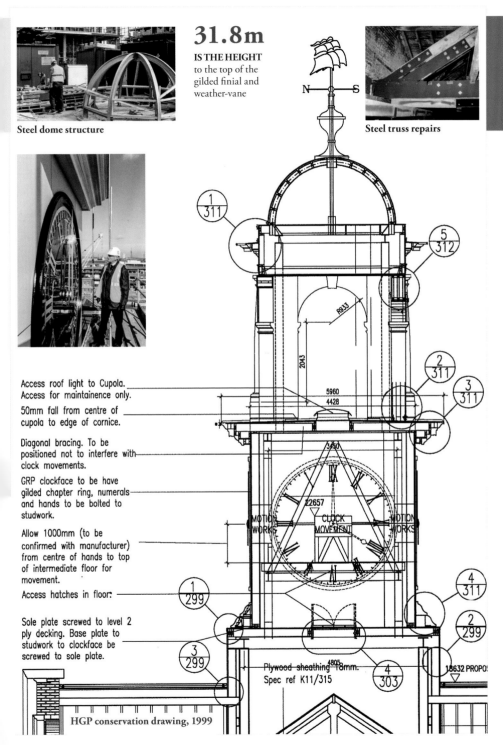

Steel dome structure

31.8m

IS THE HEIGHT
to the top of the
gilded finial and
weather-vane

Steel truss repairs

Access roof light to Cupola.
Access for maintainence only.

50mm fall from centre of
cupola to edge of cornice.

Diagonal bracing. To be
positioned not to interfere with
clock movements.

GRP clockface to be have
gilded chapter ring, numerals
and hands to be bolted to
studwork.

Allow 1000mm (to be
confirmed with manufacturer)
from centre of hands to top
of intermediate floor for
movement.

Access hatches in floor.

Sole plate screwed to level 2
ply decking. Base plate to
studwork to clockface be
screwed to sole plate.

Plywood sheathing 18mm.
Spec ref K11/315

HGP conservation drawing, 1999

165

Developing the east end

Berkeley had been planning the development at the eastern end of the site well before the 2001 opening of Gunwharf Quays

A two acre (0.8 hectare) site had been identified already for two hotels; but Berkeley also wanted to demolish the once-listed Ariadne wardroom building and develop it and the gardens in front. It was earmarked as Retail Phase II as early as 1998.

Although there was heated debate over the historic value of Ariadne and the viability of its repair and future use, in the end, Conservation Area Consent for its demolition was obtained in April 2000, along with permission for a 4,600 sq m (50,000 sq ft) office building on the Ariadne footprint.

Meanwhile, residential construction continued south of the canal well after 2001 and the Waterfront apartments were completed in 2002. The Canalside apartments, with ground floor retail units opening up the south side of the canal, commenced that year.

Ariadne site

After approval was given in 2004 for a hotel and shops extension to the completed retail/leisure complex on the gardens site (keeping Donegal Lodge), permission was granted for the Round House development of more than 160 apartments, with 126 for 'key workers' and a nursery (now a supermarket). This replaced the offices proposal and required the demolition of Donegal.

The Plaza

The provision of a hotel on this site had the effect of releasing the large two acre site for other development. Berkeley submitted a scheme for a 29-storey residential tower block (No.1 Gunwharf Quays) with lower adjoining blocks (the Crescent and the Blue Building), around to the southern entrance, providing 315 apartments. After an initial application in 2003, the final scheme was approved in 2005 and work on site commenced in 2006. Restaurants and cafés occupy some of the ground floors.

From left to right: Hotel, Round House and No.1

Constructing East Plaza, 2007

Cafés and apartments overlooking The Plaza

From left: **Blue Building, The Crescent, No. 1 (Broadway Malyon), Ariadne Building (The Amos Partnership), Round House (Broadway Malyon)**

The tower, known locally as the 'lipstick' because of its oval form and diagonal top, is a well-designed landmark building at the eastern end of the canal and a successful architectural counter-point to the Spinnaker Tower.

Two additional architectural practices, The Amos Partnership, and (the now global) Broadway Malyon, were brought in to design the buildings at the east end of the site.

The Plaza and Ariadne sites, constructed after 2001, formed significant additional property development, adding over 480 dwellings to the 310 in the original 1998 permission. This maximised the development potential of Gunwharf Quays.

Computer-generated image of No 1, Gunwharf Quays

The Spinnaker Tower

'I think the interesting question is why does man want to build to the sky.' American architect, Philip Johnson, (1906-2005)

Oxford may be a 'city of dreaming spires' but Portsmouth is a city of proud towers including the Round Tower, Square Tower, the Cathedral tower, Gunwharf's Vulcan clocktower; and now soaring over them all, The Spinnaker Tower.

Spinnaker Tower has become an icon of Portsmouth and the south coast of England. A true landmark in every sense - it can be seen for miles around from all directions and, sited in the harbour surrounded by Portsmouth's great naval history, it boldly signifies a new forward looking modern era for the city and the surrounding area. Part of Gunwharf Quays and just a short walk from the historic dockyard, the tower provides the city with another international tourist attraction, boosting the economy and creating a feel-good factor for local people. Importantly, its design was chosen by the people of Portsmouth and Gosport.

It was a major element in the success of the Renaissance of Portsmouth Harbour bid for Millennium Lottery funding:

'The Tower was what excited the Commission, particularly its then chairwoman, Virginia Bottomley. The scheme was exciting because it had a landmark feature which was millennial'
Millennium Commission

Spinnaker's elegant shape rises 170m out of Portsmouth Harbour. Visitors stepping out of the lift onto the large viewing platform at 100m are bowled over by the breathtaking 300 degrees vista - the merging of sea and sky, the light which changes by the hour, views of Spice Island, Gosport, the Isle of Wight, and the ferries and other shipping coming and going to the island and to mainland Europe and beyond. Closer in, there is a bird's-eye view of Portsmouth's Historic Dockyard, Nelson's *Victory*, the Mary Rose Museum, and the *Warrior*. The modern naval base and its 21st century warships lie beyond. In the distance, Chichester Cathedral and the New Forest can be seen. A glass floor - one of the largest in Europe - looking straight down to ground level adds to the excitement for those not scared of heights. At night the views are spectacular.

But the construction of this truly remarkable engineering achievement was fraught with problems - political, financial and constructional - and the people of Portsmouth became very sceptical and disillusioned with the whole process as the costs escalated and the years seemed to drag on.

The following pages tell the story of this great tower.

Spinnaker under construction

Designing the tower

January 1997 to June 1998
Architects: HGP; Engineers: LAP

The idea of a tower came from the directors of HGP out of a brainstorming session on the Portsmouth Harbour Renaissance project in 1995. The possibility of a bridge between Portsmouth and Gosport had been talked about for some time but they agreed this was unrealistic, largely because of naval access. Out of this came the idea of a water arch or arc with a tower as one of the abutments. In the end the arc part of the idea was abandoned but the tower remained.

Other members of the Renaissance team may also have had ideas for a tower but it was Peter Warlow, an HGP director, who went on to design Spinnaker. Contrary to the consultation presentations (right), his design was not inspired by a spinnaker sail but by the integration of space, form and function. Peter's wife, Gaynor, thought it looked like a spinnaker sail and the name stuck.

In late January 1997 Berkeley expressed an interest in constructing the tower, and approached HGP and international practices including civil engineers Ove Arup, German tower engineers Leonhardt, Andrae und Partner (LAP), Michael Wilford and Santiago Calatrava, for designs.

LAP insisted on working with the Gunwharf master-planners HGP. This partnership had the advantage that it met the criterion for an international team. Armed with his own design ideas, including 'Spinnaker', Peter Warlow set off to Stuttgart to meet LAP's Peter Andrae. By March the two men had developed a range of designs, including three using multiple shafts, differing from the usual symmetry and simple structural nature of LAP's tall telecommunications towers.

Cost estimates for 3 options (assuming commencement April 1998)	£m
Spinnaker	13.5
Globe	11.8
Triple Tower	11.7

The Spinnaker

The inspiration for this design is the sail. The open structured body is designed to billow out over the water, responding to its location and context, with the Solent and Portsmouth Harbour being at the heart of sailing in the UK.

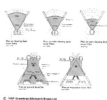

© HGP Greentree Alichurch Evans Ltd

1. Peter Warlow 2. Peter Andrae
3. Hedley Greentree and his 1966 design project with its tower for Southsea Common

Proposals by all competing practices were presented to Berkeley in April 1997 and LAP/HGP and their designs were selected.

In September, the Berkeley/LAP/HGP team was selected by Portsmouth Harbour Renaissance Ltd (led by Portsmouth City Council) with Millennium Commission agreement. It was instructed to develop three designs - the Spinnaker, the Globe and the Triple Tower.

The Fernsehturm, Stuttgart. The world's first concrete TV tower, Stuttgart, Germany, designed in 1956 by LAP

Millennium Tower project, Tokyo, designed by Fosters, 1989

The Globe

The Globe Tower is designed as a gateway and its design imagery is derived from the concept of a globe supported on twin arms bridging between Portsmouth & Gosport across Portsmouth Harbour.

It is symbolic of the many voyages of adventure and trade that have set out from this location throughout this last Millennium.

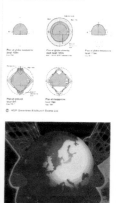

The Triple Tower

The Triple Tower derives its name directly from its three supporting shafts.
Its design imagery is industrial dockside and invokes images of the bridge of the Royal Navy ships passing close by.

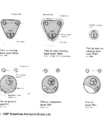

A landmark project at risk

*'A deepening cash crisis and differences of opinion...
a landmark project at risk'*
The News, Portsmouth, 15 July 1998

A public competition

A tower competition had been suggested at an early stage, not least by former government minister and Millennium Commission chairman Virginia Bottomley. However it was agreed, in view of the 2000 deadline, that it was better to have the competition between three 'outstanding business-led' design options instead of competing designers. So the public were asked to choose between the Spinnaker, the Globe and the Triple Tower.

A special February 1998 edition of Portsmouth City Council's *Flagship* publicised the three towers and the public vote. There were exhibitions, with scheme models, at the Mountbatten Gallery, Portsmouth, and Gosport Museum. Early in March the council announced that, by a good majority, the people of Portsmouth and Gosport had selected the Spinnaker design.

A difficult period for the tower

However, Berkeley had received a report from Venture Consultancy showing expected visitor numbers of 300,000 to 350,000 per year, much lower than the 1995 Touche Ross figure of nearly 700,000, and became very concerned about the financial viability of the project. They were also having doubts about proceeding with this type of venture as it was unrelated to their core business as developers. Additionally, the city council was insisting that the tower had to be completed by the year 2000. There was further work into April on a business plan for the tower and strenuous efforts were made by Portsmouth Harbour Renaissance Ltd to improve the financial position of the project. Suggestions for cost savings by eliminating public access were made by Berkeley.

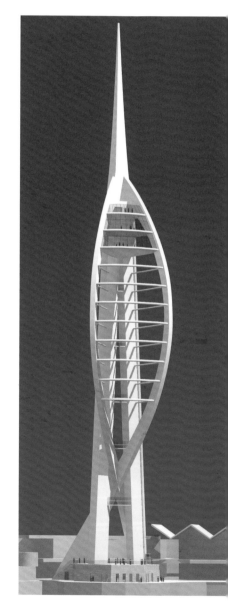

June 1998 was a particularly difficult month. Firstly, the Millennium Commission, having agreed to give around £9m towards the cost (which rose from £19m to £21m during 1998) insisted that the structure must have public access.

Then, Berkeley announced that it had decided to withdraw from the design and construction of the tower and reduced its financial contribution from nearly £10m to £3m. This was a big blow for the project. Berkeley's Roger Lewis sought to calm the situation by saying: "We're still committed to the Gunwharf scheme including the tower and other millennium features and we've assured the city council that we'll fully co-operate with them ensuring that Gunwharf will be a successful development".

The sense of crisis was heightened further by the Millennium Commission adding a warning that all the renaissance funding would be in jeopardy if the important landmark tower failed to materialise.

"The Government...believes that the Millennium Commission has made the right decision in agreeing to support the Renaissance of Portsmouth Harbour and [it hopes] that the negotiations will soon be resolved in the interests of the people of Portsmouth and Gosport".
Janet Anderson, Under-Secretary of State for Culture, Media and Sport: 2 November 1998

The need for a new tower developer

There were urgent discussions about reducing the height of the tower by up to 30m, possibly saving £2m. But, more importantly, the council and PHRL needed to find a tower developer willing to inject at least £7m.

All this was in addition to a vociferous local lobby against the whole idea of building of the tower (such as a telephone poll reported in *The News* - 513 against; 242 for) and the clamour for a public inquiry. There were also various arguments about building the tower between the parties involved. At around this time Berkeley completed the purchase of the Gunwharf site.

'It comes a no surprise that the patience of the would-be developers of Gunwharf is wearing thin, The Berkeley Group is not only now facing problems with the millennium tower but is also being frustrated over the redevelopment of the entire Gunwharf site. Investing in such an enormous eye-catching project was never going to be easy, particularly when it meant the public and private sectors working so closely.' The News 15 July 1998

Left: The News, 15 July 1998

A new company for the tower project

November 1998 to January 2000
Engineers: LAP; Architects: HGP

Following the Berkeley withdrawal from the tower project, a search was on for two developers: one for the detail design and building, and one for financing and operating the tower. Additional features were proposed to make the Tower more financially viable. HGP submitted a planning application on behalf of Portsmouth City Council for the Spinnaker Tower, to include:
- three viewing platforms,
- a panoramic lift,
- a drop ride
- five floors at the base for visitor facilities, entertainment and leisure.

Constructional design and build tenders had to follow a specification requiring a 165m high tower with a design life of 80 years.

A new company

Bids were received from international and UK companies. Some of the bidders formed a consortium: Bouygues, a French construction/telecommunications company joined with local contractors, Warings; IAF/Intamin joined leisure company, Heritage Projects. The four companies agreed to work together to part-finance, construct and operate the tower.

As a result a new company was formed - Portsmouth Spinnaker Tower Ltd (PSTL) - with a commitment to invest £12m into the project, the remaining funding coming from the Millennium Commission and Berkeley. The council was anxious not to use public funds but established a contingency fund of £600,000 to cover PSTL costs should the project fail. The Tower cost had now risen to around £28m.

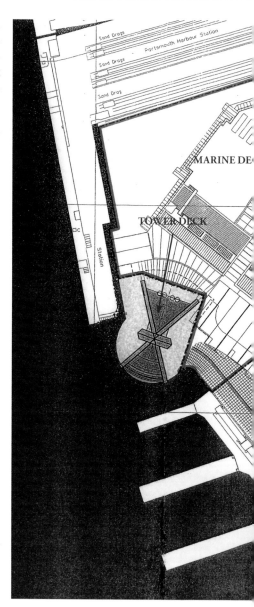

2013

WAS THE YEAR
Bouygues UK completed
the Mary Rose Museum
(right) - part of the
Portsmouth Harbour
Renaissance vision

Mary Rose Museum

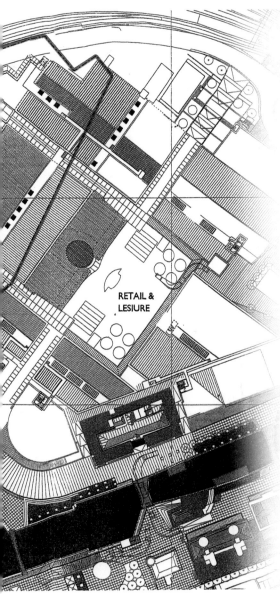

RETAIL &
LESIURE

TWA Order

The site chosen for the tower was still under water in the harbour. Application for a second Transport and Works Act Order (similar to the one for the marine deck) to allow construction of the tower and its foundation raft was made in December 1998.

Failure

Following Millennium Commission approval and a September 1999 planning permission, the big plan was for PSTL to enter into a contract with Portsmouth City Council before the end of the year, commence construction in February 2000 and achieve tower completion by summer of 2001. Unfortunately, financial unease arising from inflation and delay in the issuing of the TWA Order, led to a breakdown in trust between the council and PSTL. Many attempts were made to keep the deal alive but in January 2000 the council terminated all discussion.

A new strategy

A new strategy had to be developed and a revised planning application was submitted for a simplified Spinnaker Tower with:
• three viewing floors,
• a panoramic external lift, and
• just two floors at the base

Despite the delays, the Millennium Commission said the project funding would not be in jeopardy providing another developer was found.

An intention to build *November 2000 to October 2001*

Contractor: John Mowlem; Engineers: Scott Wilson (initially Ove Arup); Architects: HGP; Architects for visitor areas: Harrington Design

Three bidding contractors were shortlisted in the search for a new developer. They were Sir Robert McAlpine Ltd; John Mowlem & Co plc and AMEC plc. Mowlem was selected in summer 2000 and finally approved by Portsmouth City Council in November as its new tower contractor.

Design
The detailed geometry of the tower, worked out in 2000, was carefully overseen by Peter Warlow, Chris Greed and others at HGP and LAP. But, during 2001, detailed structural and construction design became the responsibility of engineers Ove Arup then, for most of the construction period, Scott Wilson.

Tower operation
Heritage Projects (later to become the Continuum Group) was selected as tower operator.

A lower cost tower and delays
A simplified Spinnaker design, at a much lower target cost, was proposed but its commencement on site was held up by funding and contractual disagreements, consultations with regulatory bodies and a delay with the TWA Order.

A letter of intent (an intention to enter into a contract) was signed by Portsmouth City Council and Mowlem. But it was not until October, 2001, eight months later, that hoardings finally went up separating the tower construction site from Gunwharf Quays, and work began.

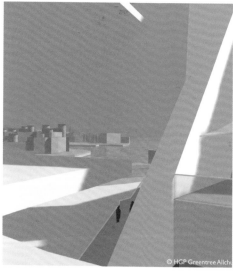

Above: **HGP computer generated images**
Right: **An LAP/HGP drawing of the Spinnaker Tower design - a key drawing for the project (March 2000)**

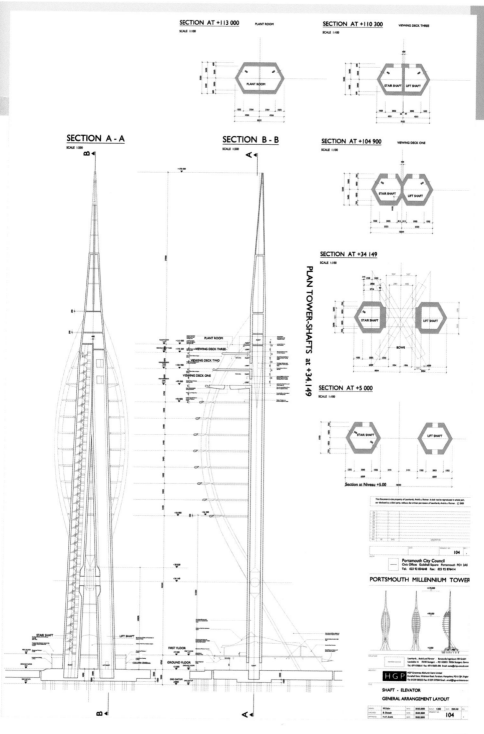

SECTION AT +113 000 PLANT ROOM
SCALE 1:100

PLANT ROOM

SECTION AT +110 300 VIEWING DECK THREE
SCALE 1:100

STAIR SHAFT LIFT SHAFT

SECTION A - A
SCALE 1:200

SECTION B - B
SCALE 1:200

SECTION AT +104 900 VIEWING DECK ONE
SCALE 1:100

STAIR SHAFT LIFT SHAFT

PLAN TOWER-SHAFTS at +34.149

SECTION AT +34 149
SCALE 1:100

STAIR SHAFT LIFT SHAFT

BOWS

SECTION AT +5 000
SCALE 1:100

STAIR SHAFT LIFT SHAFT

Section at Niveau +5.00

PLANT ROOM
VIEWING DECK THREE
VIEWING DECK TWO
VIEWING DECK ONE

STAIR SHAFT   LIFT SHAFT

FIRST FLOOR
COLUMN 2000mm
GROUND FLOOR

104

Portsmouth City Council
Civic Offices Guildhall Square Portsmouth PO1 2AS
Tel: 023 92 834648 Fax: 023 92 876414

PORTSMOUTH MILLENNIUM TOWER

Leonhardt, Andrä und Partner Beratende Ingenieure VBI GmbH
Lenbachstr.10 70180 Stuttgart · HO 100003 70056 Stuttgart, Germany
Tel.: 0711/5506-0 Fax: 0711/5605-300 E-mail: name@lap-consult.com

HGP HGP Greentree AllchurchSaare Limited
Parnshall Farm, Wickham Road, Fareham, Hampshire, PO14 QN, England
Tel: 01329 583533 Fax: 01329 537000 E-mail: email@aparchitects.com

SHAFT - ELEVATOR
GENERAL ARRANGEMENT LAYOUT

104

Construction commences - piling and a concrete raft for the Tower

Piling: October 2001 to May 2002; Raft: June 2002 to May 2003

In August 2001 there was good news: the Millennium Commission reallocated £1.6m to the Tower and a vital Infrastructure Agreement with Berkeley was signed. Portsmouth City Council decided construction had to commence but could not yet agree contractual terms with Mowlem: a revised 'letter of intent' was signed but attracted considerable criticism as it appeared to favour the contractor.

Piling started and 84 steel tube piles, each up to 50 metres long, were driven into the harbour bed and filled with reinforcement and concrete.

After piling, a pre-cast concrete raft, 2.5 - 3m deep, was built on the pile heads, the whole assembly being consolidated with reinforced concrete (concrete poured into moulds - 'shuttering' - around steel reinforcement 'cages').

In October 2002, the council appointed a project manager enabling a risk-sharing contract* to be signed. This contract shared the financial risks between the council and Mowlem

*Engineering and Construction Contract, 2nd Edition, Option C: Target Contract with Activity Schedule

in an agreed proportion and was designed to encourage good management, trust and co-operation. It ended the risks and uncertainty of the 'letter of intent' arrangement.

Piles being delivered

Raft under construction

The concrete shafts
June 2003 to October 2003

A remarkable technique called slip-forming, normally used for internal lift and stair towers, was used to construct Spinnaker's two hexagonal shafts, converging upwards at an angle of 2.4 degrees.

A £250,000, 60 tonne, 'rig', its three-storey steel casing containing adjustable timber shuttering boxes, moved gradually upwards using 28 synchronised, 6-tonne hydraulic jacks fixed to the structure, allowing the continuous pouring of carefully mixed concrete. The shafts ascended at 2 metres/working day (with about four adjustment 'breaks'). Subcontractors were cooling-tower specialists Bierrum and Partners.

The slip-form rig in progress

The shafts converge 71 metres above ground level. A 150mm cant was built into the height of the shafts so that when loaded with the steel 'spinnaker' bows the structure became vertical. Because the external concrete surface produced by slip-forming is quite rough, 2mm external Sika rendering was applied soon after the formwork had moved upwards.

Although completed only a month late, there were some problems. High winds caused difficulties; then, in September 2003, just before completion, Bierrum went into receivership. Mowlem completed the final stages.

Project Manager David Greenhalgh commented:
"The obvious risk was falls - people falling from heights and materials falling onto people, particularly during construction of the concrete shafts. Measures included fully walling the working areas of the rig with plywood, installing fine catch netting under the whole of the rig, fully enclosing it with cover sheets, providing a fully-enclosed access hoist for materials and people, and erecting a scaffold catch fan (for falling materials) at the base. These measures were agreed four months before the rig came to site."

The tower shafts being rendered

Steel bows, ribs and spacers, and the viewing decks

November 2003 to January 2005

The steel 'bows' weigh 1,200 tonnes and were made by Butterley Engineering Ltd from 52 main sections. The 35 components of the 95 tonne, 54-metres high, cruciform section were assembled at ground level using special trestles; major modules travelled by road from Derbyshire with police escorts. A large 'trunnion pin' (a box girder on bridge bearings to allow movement) connects the cruciform section to the twin concrete shafts 35 metres above ground level. The 'strand-jacking' process (hydraulic jacks working with highly-tensioned steel ropes) was used to raise the lower bow sections. One of the tallest free-standing tower cranes ever assembled placed the upper bows, then the spacers and ribs.

The bows, with eight aerofoil-shaped steel ribs between them and tubular spacers running back to the concrete shafts, help the tower act as a safe, statically simple, structure. The final section was fitted in September 2004.

Reinforced concrete viewing decks, supported on a grid of steel beams, are at 99.9m, 104.9m and 110.3m above ground level, the lowest one having the glass viewing floor. Crowning the tower is a 27 metres high glass-reinforced plastic spire.

There was a serious eight-month delay to the original three-month programme for the bow structure caused by unexpected difficulties in finalising detailed design, and procurement, fabrication, assembly, and completion stages. As with the concrete shafts, bad weather and high winds did not help.

The Butterley Company, Derbyshire, originated in 1790 and developed from mineral extraction and ironworks into a major engineering manufacturer, building the workers town Ironville. By the 1950s it employed 10,000 workers. Later it was split into three companies(Engineering, Bricks, and Aggregates); the huge sheds of Butterley Engineering dominated the company's site in the 1980s up to its demise in 2009. Other Butterley projects: HMS *Warrior* deck beams (1860), St Pancras roof structure (1866), and more recently, the Falkirk Wheel canal boat lift (a millennium project).

Cruciform bow section in place

Rib   Bow   Spacers

Bow section being hoisted

Final bow section being lowered into place

Viewing decks under construction

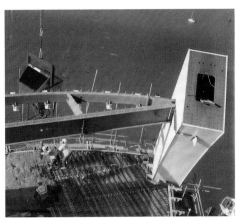

Steelwork and concreting to viewing decks

Scaffolding to viewing decks

Connecting lightweight spire to top of concrete tower

Viewing decks, lifts and completion

February to October 2005

Maspero lift car

Structural bolted glazing for the three tiered observation decks was designed and made by Winchester company, Lakesmere. Bearing-supported glass fins were designed to carry the weight of the sloping glass assemblies, with special sliding connections accommodating the anticipated movements of the tower.

The internal lift, manufactured and installed by the Finnish company Kone, carries 26 passengers at 4m/second allowing access to Viewing Deck 1 in 28 seconds.

An inclined external glass lift, ascending one of the sloping shafts by a simple rack and pinion system, had been proposed and was designed by engineers Halcrow, HGP and a Swedish lift company. However, the sub-contractor employed by Mowlem, an Italian company, Maspero Elevatori, used a system of cables rather than rack and pinion. Work progressed and in June 2005 Maspero declared the lift installation complete and working. Disappointingly, a team of lift experts found numerous defects. Breakdowns occurred, including at the tower's opening on 18 October, and in the end the external lift was abandoned.

Since its opening in 2005 Spinnaker Tower has been a massive success. The £35m tower attracts visitors from all around the world who can look out on a fascinating and historically significant panorama. State of the art lighting techniques transform Spinnaker after dark into a fabulous shining beacon that can be seen for miles around. It is a truly iconic building which is representative of Portsmouth all over the world.

Fitting the glazing

Construction operatives on viewing deck

Braving the largest glass floor in Europe at Spinnaker!

There is a silver lining to the external lift story. The tower has now become a popular abseiling destination and, where the lift would have been, around 1,800 people each year make the 94m (308ft) decent raising many thousands of pounds for charities.

Picture Credits

The author has made every effort to contact copyright holders and will be happy to correct, in subsequent editions, any errors or omissions that are brought to his attention.

Architecture PLB 134 (1,2)

Berkeley Group 11 (centre right), 94-95 (lower), 112-113 (Peter Hutton), 124-125 (central), 130-131 (central), 132-133 (perspectives - Peter Hutton and other artist(s)), 138 (lower left), 141 (top central), 156 (lower left), 166 (lower left), 167 (right), 176-177

British Library 16-17, 26-27, 29 (top right), 30-31 (plan), 37 (top), 38(centre left), 40-41 (top), 44-45

CJB Photography 96-97, 148-149, 150-151, 152-153, 156-157, 158-159

Continuum Group [Heritage Projects (Portsmouth) Ltd] 9 (lower), 167 (upper left), 170, 180 (lower), 181, 183 (upper, middle right, lower right), 184 (upper), 185 (upper, lower left)

CZWG Architects 134-35 (6)

English Heritage Archive 34-35 (plans, sections), 36-37 (plan), 41 (plan, section), 42 (section), 43 (lower left), 58 (top), 59 (plans), 74-75 (lower section, not ROF), 83 (top)

Explosions Museum, Gosport 77 (bottom), 78

Fred Aldsworth 38 (plan), 42 (plan), 69 (plan), 129 (plans)

Foster and Partners 173 (top right)

Google Cultural Institute (courtesy National Gallery of Art, Washington DC) 49 (top left)

Gunwharf Quays Management Ltd. (Land Securities) 8 (upper right), 15, 96, 148-149, 152-153 (main photograph), 156-157 (main photograph), 158-159 (main photograph)

HGP Architects 39 (top), 62-63 (lower), 94 (top),94-95 (top upper), 101, 111 (right), 118-119 (PLC), 122, 133 (bottom right), 134-135 (4,7), 138 (upper right), 161 (top,middle left), 165 (right), (lower), 172-173, 174, 175, 178, (179)

Hopkins Architects 100 (lower)

Hutton and Rostron Environmental Investigations Ltd 163 (upper)

Hutton, Peter 112-113, 132 (top left), 133 (top right)

John Thompson and Partners 136-137 (except photograph)

Lakesmere Ltd 182, 183 (middle and lower left), 184 (lower left and right)

Leonhardt, Andrae und Partner 173 (top centre right) 179

MacMillan and Co. Ltd 95 (centre right)

Myles Waterman 11 (upper right), 141 (top right), 146-147 (main photograph)

National Archives 23 (lower), 29 (lower), 48-49 (plan), 50-51, 52 (plan), 53 (sections), 55 (upper), 60 (lower), 61 (except location), 64-65 (sections), 72-73, 74-75 (upper section, ROF plan), 76, 77 (left side), 78-79, 91 (lower)

National Portrait Gallery 66 (bottom left)

News, The (Portsmouth) 93 (top), 109, 158 (top left), 175 (bottom left)

Pete Clutterbuck (and John Duffield), blacksmiths 39 (right)

PLC Architects plans inside covers

Portsmouth City Archives 65 (top three right)

Portsmouth City Council 111 (top left)

Portsmouth City Library 25 (upper left), 39 (lower), 43 (centre), 46-47, 56, 68

Portsmouth City Museums 8 (right)

Portsmouth Royal Dockyard Trust Support Group 99 (lower)

Proctor and Matthews 134-135 (3,5)

Raphilena Bonito 18 (lower left), 22(lower), 40-41 (lower)

3DReid (formerly Geoffrey Reid Associates) 132-133 (elevations, central and upper), 1399 (lower left), 140-141 (central), 142-143 (plan), 150 (lower left), 152 (lower left), 158 (upper left), 168-169

Richard Thomas 150-151 (main photograph), 155

Robert Kennedy 32-33, 52-53, 63 (upper right), 95 (top), 139 (upper left), 143 (top right)

Roedean School, Sussex 90 (centre right)

The News, Portsmouth 93 (top), 106-107 (centre), 173 (top centre), 175 (lower)

UK Hydrographic Office 21 (centre)

University of Texas Libraries at Austin (by courtesy) 66 (portrait lower centre)

Wikimedia Commons 21 (top left), 29 (top left), 43 (right, below photo: CC-BY-SA3.0), 79 (top), 87 (right), 108-109 (bottom: CC-BY-SA2.0), 109 (bottom centre: Christine Matthews CC-BY-SA2.0), 114-115 (lower: Coda, Coza CC-BY-SA2.0), Colin Smith (CC-BY-SA2.0) 39 (middle left)

Acknowledgements

This book arose in part out of three years from 1998 directing the repair of historic buildings at Gunwharf Quays. It was also inspired by two talks: the first was by Peter Emery, a former Centre Manager at Gunwharf Quays, the other by Stephen Baily, Portsmouth's Head of City Development and Cultural Services.

From the outset my wife, Julie, made the decision to join me as editor in this venture. A quick look around the local bookshops and on-line assured us that no-one else had had the idea first – there was no book to be found on Gunwharf Quays.

We had a very positive meeting with Stephen Baily, and David Evans, at Portsmouth Civic Offices in March 2013 and were directed to Tricorn Books in the High Street, Portsmouth. Its two directors Gail Baird and Dan Barnard, not only became our publishers but a source of wisdom, encouragement and sheer enthusiasm, brilliantly executing the final design of our embryonic pages over the next two years.

Other encouragements in the early months came from Piers Gorman and Mike Davidson of Land Securities, owners of the retail/leisure sector of Gunwharf Quays, from Tony Pidgley, Chairman of the Berkeley Group, the developers of Gunwharf Quays, and from director Peter Warlow, of HGP Architects. Peter kindly gave access to the HGP archives. Claire Upton-Brown, Portsmouth City Council Head of Planning, gave access, assisted by Wendy Mitchell, to the planning archives. Lindy Elliott and her librarians were a great help in the Portsmouth Central Library and Katie Ball guided me through the relevant documents and artefacts held in the Portsmouth Archives. The efficiency of, and assistance at, the National Archives, the British Library and the English Heritage Archives are also gratefully acknowledged. Others who contributed were Jo Bushnell, Dr Ann Coates, Mike Coulter, Explosions Museum, Gosport, Ian Froome, Stephen Hedges, Graham Hickson-Smith, Lt. Comm. Rob Hoole, Alistair and Yvonne Hunt, Mo Morgan, Chris Owen, Sue Pike, David Sherren, Ellie Stokes, Anne Vail, Kathy Wadsworth, Simon Wildgust and Colin Wilding. We are grateful for the results of the artistic skills of Raphilena Bonito and Rob Kennedy.

We received a huge amount of help from some who had been personally involved in the transformation of a derelict MoD site into the Gunwharf Quays of today. Without exception they remembered their time at Gunwharf with enthusiasm and were eager to contribute. They include, in addition to those mentioned above, Fred Aldsworth, Tony Allies, Peter Andrae, Trevor Blow, Neale Brickwood, David Brock, Peter Goodship, Hedley Greentree, Chris Hacking, Steven Hassel, John Hyland, David Lakeland, Jeremy Lear, Roger Lewis, Phil Parkinson, John Pike, Sarah Royle-Johnson, Paul Spooner, Lord Stoneham, Richard Thomas, Rob Tincknell, and Myles Waterman.

We thank everyone for their valued help and encouragement.

Above all, I want to thank Julie, my wife, for not only acting and surviving as editor for the last two years but much more. She has played a profoundly beneficial role in every aspect of the book. Without her it would have been very different and, I strongly suspect, a much less interesting volume.

Michael Underwood

Bibliography

Anon. (2004). Berkeley's Gunwharf Quays development in Portsmouth. *Housebuilder*, Vol.63, Pt 4, 39-40.

Ashurst, J. (See Hutton and Rostron).

Aldsworth, F. (see The Conservation Practice)

Berkeley Group plc (in association with Lordland CC (SA)). (1996). *An Expression of Interest in the Development Opportunities at Gunwharf Quay, Portsmouth*. Cobham: The Berkeley Group plc. (bid to Secretary of State for Defence)

Berry, W. (2013). *The Pre-Dreadnought Revolution*. Stroud: The History Press.

Board of Ordnance A/C1713-1714 http://www.british-history.ac.uk/report.aspx?compid=86106

Burton, L. (1992). *Feeding the Forces: The History of Royal Clarence Yard, 1827-1992*. Gosport: The Gosport Society.

Butcher, T. K, (1973). *The Navy*. London: B. T. Batsford Ltd.

Coad, J. (1981). *Historic Architecture of HM Naval Base, Portsmouth: 1700-1850*. Portsmouth: the Portsmouth RN Museum Trading Co. Ltd.

Coad, J, (1989). *The Royal Dockyards 1690-1850*. Aldershot: Scholar Press.

Coad, J, (2013). *Support for the Fleet*. London: English Heritage.

Conservation Practice, The. (1997). *Gunwharf Quays, Portsmouth: An Archaeological Evaluation*. Midhurst: The Conservation Practice.

Corney, A. (1965). *Fortifications in Old Portsmouth*. Portsmouth: Portsmouth City Museums.

Cousins, R. (2014). *A Brief History of Leigh Park and the Hamlet of Leigh*. (with other sections)

Crocker, G. (1999). *The Gunpowder Industry*. (2nd ed.). Oxford: Shire Publications Ltd.

Curl, J. S. (2006). *Oxford Dictionary of Architecture and Landscape Architecture*. Oxford: Oxford University Press

Cunliffe, B. (1977). *Excavations at Portchester Castle*. London: The Society of Antiquaries.

David Lock Associates (with HGP Greentree Allchurch Evans Ltd, Geoffrey Reid Associates, Hyland Edgar Driver). (1997). *Gunwharf Quays, Portsmouth: Folio of Illustrations for Development Statement*.

David Lock Associates (with others). (1997). *Gunwharf Quays, Portsmouth: Supporting Illustrations for Development Statement*.

Dicker, S. (1972). *HMS Vernon Centenary: A Short History of the Establishment*. Portsmouth: HMS Vernon.

Dixon, T. J, & Marston, A. (2003). *Mixed use urban regeneration at Bradley Place, Birmingham, and Gunwharf Quays, Portsmouth: an assessment of the impact on local and national economies*. Reading: College of Estate Management.

Downing, T. (2010). *Churchill's War Lab*. London: Little, Brown.

Evans, D. (2001). *Priddy's Hard: a historical assessment*.

Evans, D. (2006). *Arming the Fleet* (The development of the Royal Ordnance Yards 1770-1945). Gosport: Explosion Museum (with English Heritage).

Gates, W. G. (1900), *Illustrated History of Portsmouth*. Portsmouth: Charpentier and Co.

Goodall, J. (2003). *Portchester Castle* (2nd ed.). London: English Heritage.

Grant, L. and Scott, D. (1996). *Waterfront developments as tools for urban reconstruction and regeneration in South Africa* (Durban). Urban Forum. 7 (2), 125-138

Henry, C. (2005). *Depth Charge!* Barnsley: Pen and Sword Military.

HGP. (1997). *Infirmary Building: Preliminary Intentions*. Fareham: HGP

HGP. (1997). *Photographic Record: Gunwharf Site, Portsmouth*. Farham: HGP

HGP. (1997). *Vernon Building: Preliminary Intentions*. Fareham: HGP

HGP. (1997). *Vulcan Building: Preliminary Intentions*. Fareham: HGP

Holman, N. E. (1999). *Networks, design and regeneration: a case study of the Gunwharf regeneration project*. Unpublished thesis, University of Portsmouth, Portsmouth.

Hutton and Rostron. (1998). *Survey of masonry and recommendations on remedial works*. Gomshall: Hutton and Rostron Environmental Investigations Ltd.

Hoyle, B. (2000). *Global and local change on the port-city waterfront*. Southampton: The University of Southampton.

King, A. (2011). *The Portsmouth Encyclopedia*. Portsmouth: Portsmouth City Council.

Lake, J. and Douet, J. (1998). *Thematic Survey of English Naval Dockyards*. London: English Heritage.

Lake, J. (2003). *Thematic Survey of the Ordnance Yards and Magazine Depots*. London: English Heritage.

Lavery, B. (2009). *Empire of the Seas*. London: Conway.

Lloyd, D. (with Pevsner, N.).(1967). *Hampshire and the Isle of Wight*. London: Penguin Books.

Morley, B. M. (1976). *Henry VIII and the Development of Coastal Defences*. London: HMSO.

Patterson, B. *Dockyard Chronology*. Retrieved 21 October 2014:
portsmouthdockyard.org.uk/Dockyard%20Chronology.pdf

Patterson, A. T. (1976). *Portsmouth: a history*. Bradford on Avon: Moonraker Press.

Pevsner's Architectural Glossary. (2010). New Haven and London: Yale University Press.

Poland, E.N. (1993). *The Torpedomen*. Portsmouth: E.N. Poland.

Pomeroy, S. *Barracks and Buildings in Portsmouth*. Retrieved 21 October 2014,
homepage.ntlworld.com/stephen.pomeroy/local/barracks.pdf

Portsmouth City Council (see Wymes)

Prior, M.D. (2014). *The Great Guns of HMS Victory*. Waterlooville: Chain-shot Books.

Pugh, M. (1956). *Commander Crabb*. London: MacMillan and Co. Ltd.

Revell, A.L. (2000). *Haslar: The Royal Hospital*. Gosport: The Gosport Society.

Ridout Associates. (1998).*Timber Decay and Damp* (at Vulcan, Vernon, Infirmary, and Lockeeper's Cottage and South Gate Buildings - 4 vols.). Hagley: Ridout Associates.

Ridout Associates. (1998). *Decay Probe Survey of Beam Ends and Truss Ends* (at Vulcan, Building). Hagley: Ridout Associates.

Rigold, S. E. (1965). *Portchester Castle* (3rd ed.) London: Her Majesty's Stationery Office.

Riley, Ray (Ed.). (2005). *Maritime City: Portsmouth 1945-2005*. Stroud: Sutton Publishing Ltd.

Riley, Ray. (2002). *Portsmouth Ships, Dockyard & Town*. Stroud: Tempus Publishing Ltd.

Rodgers, S. (2000). The Seamaster: The Gunwharf. Portsmouth: Anti-Subarine Warfare Instructors Association

Rowley-Williams, L. (1998). *Infirmary Watching Brief; Gunwharf Quays, Portsmouth*. Southampton: Gifford and Partners

Sadden, J. (2001). *Portsmouth: In Defence of the Realm*. Chichester: Philimore and Co. Ltd.

Sayer, G.B. (1930). *HMS Vernon: A history*. Portsmouth: The Mess Committee, Wardroom Mess, HMS Vernon.

Semark, H.W. (2001). *The Royal Naval Armament Depots of Priddy's Hard et al (Gosport, Hampshire) 1768 to 1977* (3rd ed.). Gosport: Museum of Naval Firepower Ltd.

Southgate, M. (1991). *The Old Tide Mill at Eling*. Eling: Eling Tide Mill Trust Ltd.

Southgate, M. (2003). *Colonel Goring's Gamble*. Apex Publications

Timbers, K. (2011) *The Royal Arsenal, Woolwich*. London : Royal Arsenal Woolwich Historical Society.

Webb, J., Yates, N., Peacock, S. (Eds.): *Hampshire Studies* (1981). Portsmouth: Portsmouth City Records Office.

Webb, E.D. (1955). *HMS Vernon: A Short History from 1930 to 1955*. Portsmouth: The Wardroom Mess Committee, HMS Vernon.

Wilson, A.W. (1944, 5th Ed.1985). *The story of the Gun*.

Winton, J. (1989). *The Naval Heritage of Portsmouth*. Southampton: Ensign Publications.

Wood, A. B. (1965). From the Board of Invention and Research to the Royal Naval Scientific Service. *Journal of the Royal Naval Scientific Service*, 20/4.

Woolfit, C. (See Hutton and Rostron).

Wymes, L.C. (1995). *Portsmouth City Local Plan*. Portsmouth: Portsmouth City Counci.

Index

Page numbers in italics refer to illustrations

About the author

Michael Underwood practiced architecture for more than forty years and has a Masters degree in Historic Building Conservation. He was project architect for most of the historic buildings at Gunwharf Quays from 1998 to 2001 and founded HGP Conservation, a specialist team within HGP Architects. A Senior Lecturer in Historic Building Conservation at the University of Portsmouth from 2004 until 2012, Michael lives in Southsea with his wife, Julie.

TRICORN
BOOKS